John Candler's (1964)

Miniature Wargames

Napoleonic Wargami~

du temps de Napoı

Edited by John Curry

There are over 80 other books edited by John Curry as part of the History of Wargaming Project. They include:

Donald Featherstone's Tank Battles in Miniatures Vol 1: A Wargaming Guide to the Western Desert Campaign 1940-1942

Bruce Quarrie's Tank Battles in Miniature Vol 2: A Wargamer's Guide to the Eastern Front 1941-45

Donald Featherstone's Battles with Model Tanks

Army Wargames: Staff College Exercises 1870-1980.

Donald Featherstone's Lost Tales

Donald Featherstone's Skirmish Wargaming

Donald Featherstone's Wargaming Campaigns

Donald Featherstone's Wargaming Commando Operations and Reflections on Wargaming

Donald Featherstone's Solo Wargaming

Paddy Griffith's Napoleonic Wargaming for Fun

Verdy's 'Free Kriegspiel' including the Victorian Army's 1896 War Game

Tony Bath's Ancient Wargaming

The Fletcher Pratt Naval Wargame

See The History of Wargaming Project at www.wargaming.co for other publications.

ISBN 978-0-244-92868-1

Cover photo Napoleonic battle using Jack Scruby Miniatures from Bob Bard (1957) *Making and Collecting Military Miniatures* Robert M. McBride Co., Inc., New York

Contents

Ohio was the centre of American wargaming for a while. This photo, taken by Tom Bookwalter, circa 1963 shows some of the key figures of the time. 1st row, left to right Dave Towell, Tom Bookwalter, Duke Seifried; 2nd row, left to right, John Candler, Gary Locker, Stan Glanzer. Duke and John Candler worked at the same television station. John Candler was a gentleman to game with. In the early 60s, there was no basing of wargame figures. They all stood on the base that was cast on the bottom of their feet! Needless to say, moving individual figures that way often resulted in a figure toppling over. When he did so, very often he took down the rest of the line. When that happened, John would always say "on your feet knuckleheads". Photo reproduced with kind permission of Tom Bookwalter.

Preface

This early set of wargaming rules was published by the author, John C Candler, in the United States in 1964. They were published in a green A5 ring binder, rather than as a traditional book, which must have reduced their impact on the emerging wargaming market. This format almost certainly reduced their chances of survival and not many copies of this work are left on old wargamers' shelves.

The comprehensive rules were charmingly illustrated with black and white photographs of Jack Scruby's 30mm Napoleonic range. The rules were supported with various historical notes, including short biographies of some key figures such as Blucher, Nelson and Wellington. Such precis of military history were invaluable in the days before the proliferation of military history books and the ubiquitous power of Google that answers practically any straightforward question on history. However, it was an easy editorial decision to make to omit these outdated sections on history.

Wargaming was in its pioneering days. Featherstone had produced the book *War Games* in 1962 for the mass market. This set of rules was clearly for the dedicated wargamer. The size of the hobby in 1964 was shown by the author including the actual names and addresses of all the 113 wargamers in the United States of whom Candler knew.

Chandler did promise further sets of rules, but sadly these were never published to my knowledge. The rules also contained a reference to *Napoleonique*, a 'Vest Pocket Wargame', complete with men, playing surface, terrain variables, maps, plotting surfaces and marking pencils. The game was designed to fit on a standard card table. The box would contain a French and British army, with 10 figures for each of the five line companies per side, two five man cavalry squadrons, two artillery batteries with a three man crew, a surgeon and afield commander: a grand total of 138 men, with four guns. The marketing plan was to have an unpainted version, a middle range version with one painted figure of each type and a set with all figures fully painted.

Unfortunately, the scale of the wargaming market in the USA was apparently insufficient to support such an off-the-shelf game in the 1960's, so the idea was never turned into an actual product. However, at the same time Waddingtons did produce a simple wargame along similar lines. *The Battle of the Little Big Horn* (1962), did contain a map with painted figures for the Indians and US Cavalry. The game is straightforward, but with mounted troops moving faster than foot, ranged attacks and different victory conditions for each side, the Waddingtons game was clearly in the wargame space. So perhaps there is the intriguing possibility that a large games company, such as the UK's Waddingtons, could have taken Candler's idea and brought a variant of it to market. My own view is if Candler's work had been published in the UK, it would have been picked up by Patrick Stephens Limited (Donald Featherstone's publisher) and gone to a second edition as a hardback book.

It is hoped that the republication of this early work makes it available again to enthusiasts who are intrigued by the development of our hobby.

John C. Candler (1928- 2012) passed away at the age of 83. He was buried in the Ft. Gibson National Cemetery.

John Curry, August 2017.

MINIATURE WARGAMES

Du temps de Napoleon

at the time of Napoleon

By John C. Candler

(1964)

Foreword

Wargaming is one of man's oldest diversions. Chess, that exercise in logic and strategy, is thought to have evolved from the wargames of ancient orientals. Tiny figures of soldiers in battle formations have been found in tombs of Egyptian nobles dating as far back as 1000 B.C.

MINIATURE WARGAMES du temps de Napoleon is written in an effort to establish universal rules for playing wargames set in the Napoleonic era. It is hoped that a table top general may travel from one locale to another and engage in a musket period wargame with a minimum of confusion over rules and procedures.

I have corresponded and conversed with many persons concerning wargames over the past several years. The need for universal procedures seemed uppermost among their thoughts. To list all those who offered help and encouragement would require several pages.

The rules and explanations herein have been devised, revised, tested and established through the most practical method possible - use in wargaming. Many games have been interrupted to discuss (sometimes quietly) the particular merits and drawbacks of a rule or application. Games have been played on terrains ranging from flat plains to highly complex countrysides with cities, valleys, mountains, rivers, forests, swamps and one highly memorable assault on an eight-contour escarpment crossing a broad open field!

Following MINIATURE WARGAMES du temps de Napoleon will be other books concerning tabletop warfare. Periods under consideration are: American Civil War, Seven Years' War, Boer War, Franco-Prussian War, Punic Wars and American Revolutionary War.

Questions and suggestions for future books or revisions in this one will be answered as fully and quickly as possible. The book is loose-leaf bound for easier use at the table, to facilitate inserting your own notes in their proper places, and to take future additions. It is requested you respect the time and expense represented in the compilation, printing, distributing and copyrighting of this book.

To the newest hobbyist - Welcome! You are entering the company of a vast number of dedicated people ranging in age from lads in their sub-teens to men in their nineties bearing sabre wounds from the Boer War – Gentlemen all! You can make friends through correspondence and gain information about your hobby. To my knowledge there is no other hobby whose participants are so eager to swap information and help the newcomer than that of wargaming and collecting military miniatures.

Cordially

John C. Candler

INDEX OF PHOTOGRAPHS

Photos were by Tom Bookwalter and Pete Nuggesser

Pen and ink sketches by Helene Mueller

Introduction

Who among us has reached puberty without entertaining the dream of commanding a great military force? We have played at war using figures on the living room rug, yelling 'bam' at each other in the back yard, and at the Chess board. Miniature wargaming is in many respects similar to Chess, yet having infinitely greater depth and opportunities for variation. With all its complexities, miniature wargaming is extremely simple and logical in application once one is familiar with the rules and procedures.

In today's military training schools we find sandtables and the various figures needed to instruct future officers in tactics and strategy necessary to Atomic warfare, a valuable holdover from pre-Atomic days.

H. G. Wells is one of many men of note who relaxed with wargames. His *Little Wars* is one of the hobby's classics. Robert Louis Stevenson wrote the *Yallowbally Journal* in which he gave accounts of battles enjoined on his living room floor or across the lawns of his estates. Both of these gentlemen were joined by statesmen, nobility, high-ranking officers, men of letters and men of science. In short, playing with 'little tin soldiers' has for many years, been a favourite pastime of kings, emperors, persons with doctorates and some who can be considered barely literate!

Miniature wargames are played with military miniatures on tabletops with terrains which may be changed to represent an historic battleground or be a result of the players' fertile imaginations. There is no gridded board, no rules of movement other than the Field Regulations and move distances patterned after the manoeuvring of the period.

During the course of the game, infantry fires volleys and charges into hand-to-hand combat; cavalry charges are launched and repelled; artillery fires explosive shells, solid round shot or canister into troop formations; wounded men are tended by the surgeons; supply wagons speed supplies and ammunition to troops and batteries; hills are won and lost, and the outcome may hinge upon a small hard-pressed group holding a vantage point until reinforcements can arrive. A seemingly impetuous charge may sweep the field clear of the enemy or previously valiant troops may suffer sudden loss of morale and desert in the face of an inferior force!

The results of combat action (musketry, hand-to-hand combat, etc.) are determined by throwing dice with the scores interpreted according to a number of simple rules. The action is extremely realistic in its effect.

Reenactments of historic battles following original actions have produced results closely parallel to actuality.

The game is designed to simulate as closely as possible the strategic considerations and evaluations made by national and military commanders in the period 1795-1815. It is intended to impart some measure of the excitement and calculation of military conflict without the disaster, death and cruelty of real war which is certainly pleasing to no sane man.

This is a game of skill, the object of which is to defeat the opponent by destroying his ability to continue whether engaged in a 'border skirmish' or an 'international war' involving several players scattered across the globe.

Measurements used herein have been established using 30mm figures on a playing surface measuring six by twelve feet. The scales are not so extreme that persons favouring 54mm or 20mm figures will have difficulty using them.

The most challenging and interesting individual battles are fought between forces of 'balanced inequality', forces having different basic compositions yet being the same in overall worth or 'points value'. The hypothetical divisions listed are based on this theory.

Bear in mind that organisational tables given are those which the author has found best within the framework of his experience and are offered as models. It is logical that all players will not have the quantity of troops required to make up these divisions or that one's existing tactical organisation may be fitted to the rules.

Miniature Wargames du Temps de Napoleon concerns itself with European continental armies of the period and their tactics. In general, the guerrilla tactics employed by the Spanish patriots could best be represented by applying the rules/limitations given for light infantry skirmishers.

The game is made realistic by having parallels to the actual equipment and functions of the various military and naval units of the Napoleonic era.

Small arms of the period had evolved from the large artillery pieces and were largely smooth-bore muskets. The few rifles in military use in Europe were in the hands of the light infantry. Other troops carried the flintlock musket with paper cartridges. The methods of loading all firearms was to bite off the end of the cartridge and pour the powder in the barrel, then ram the ball in on the top of the charge, prime the pan and hope the projectile went in the general direction of the enemy.

Infantrymen went into battle carrying about sixty cartridges in their cartouches strung together in packets of 10-15. Since humidity, unstable chemical elements, age and broken flints were factors, a 20% misfire was considered low! All muskets were approximately the same calibre and weighed about 9 ¾ pounds.

'Plug' bayonets had been discontinued by this time in favour of ring-mounted bayonets which permitted firing with the bayonet in place.

Effective musket range was about 255 yards when fired at level sight. When aimed carefully the musket was accurate up to about 135 yards. Rifles had an effective range of about 350 yards and were considered accurate up to about 200 yards. Pistols were in use but have little importance in the game.

In addition to muskets, infantrymen were issued sabres or short swords. Sabres issued to Engineers were usually serrated on the back edge for use as light saws.

Small arms were referred to as: Muskets, Rifles, Musketoons, Carbines (carried by Dragoons, Engineers and Supply personnel) and sometimes blunderbusses were found in use.

Field artillery had been standardised into 4 pound horse and field guns, 8 and 12- pound field guns and 6-inch howitzers. Mortars will not figure in our game. Naval, coastal (fort) and siege guns ranged much heavier and will be discussed in their proper sections.

Four, eight and twelve pounders fired solid roundshot or canister. Howitzers fired explosive shells and canister.

Rockets were becoming a part of field ordnance. True, rockets did not inflict much damage but they played decisive roles in the battles of Boulogne (1806), Copenhagen (1807), Walcheren (1807), Adour (1813), Leipzig (1813) and Bladensburg (1814). Rockets of the period were the Congreve type and were armed with explosive heads and impact fused. Rockets were usually fired at emplaced troops as anti-morale weapons, there were instances of green levies breaking under heavy concentrations, and no horse in its right mind would stand while these gadgets blazed a few feet over its head. Rockets would also be launched at artillery or supply depots attempting to start fires.

'Grenadiers' in this period, and in our game, are the elite companies of infantry rather than 'grenade throwers'. With increased musket range and accuracy it became more than risky to throw the somewhat harmless grenades of former years, although the Dutch had invented a grenade-launching musketoon many years earlier.

Game Mechanics

Organisational Tables

One of the most-asked questions is: 'How many men do I need to play the game?' The best answer I can give is: 'Any number over fifty on each side, as long as opposing forces are fairly matched in value and basic unit strength'. The concept of wargaming used in this book is that each model represents one man rather than a squad, company, battalion or other unit. True, it is a bit hard to field armies numbering in the thousands but you will find that two armies with a total of 600 men will resemble a campaign before the game is ended.

As a rule-of-thumb I offer the following Tactical Organisational tables:

Infantry

Squad	5 men
Company	10 men = 2 Squads
Battalion	20 men = 2 Companies plus Officer, Flags, Drummer and NCO (optional)
Regiment	40 men = 2 Battalions
Brigade	120 men = 3 Regiments
Corps	240 men = 2 Brigades
Army	720 men = 3 Corps plus Officers

Cavalry

Troop	5 mounted men
Squadron	10 mounted men = 2 Troops
Regiment	30 mounted men = 3 Squadrons

Artillery

Battery*	5 men with 1 gun, limber and horses
Regiment*	20 men in 4 Batteries
Rocket Battery	3 men with 1 launcher, 1 pack horse

Rocket Regiment   15 men with 5 launchers, 5 pack horses

*Horse or Field Artillery

Special Services

Squad   5 Engineers

Company   10 Engineers = 2 Squads

Battalion   20 Engineers = 2 Companies

Supply Squad   2 men, 1 wagon, horses

Supply Battalion   10 men, 5 wagons, horses

Medical Officer   (Staff optional)

Field Commander   (Staff optional)

The basic tactical group is the 10 man Company. The smallest group of Line Infantry which may operate independently is a 5 man Squad which is available to serve as Artillery or Supply replacements or as prisoner escorts or guards.

Hypothetical Divisional Composition

For newcomers to the game, or for those who are not familiar with the concept of 'balanced inequality', the following hypothetic divisional types are offered.

Raider Division:

15 units Light Infantry

8 units Light Infantry Rifles

30 units Line Infantry

4 units Foot Guard

3 units Engineers*

7 units Light Cavalry

5 units Heavy Cavalry

2 units Guard Infantry

4 units Horse Artillery

3 units 8-pound Field Artillery

2 units 6-inch Howitzers

3 units Rocket Corps

1 Surgeon

1 Field Commander

Field Offensive Division:

8 units Light Infantry

2 units Light Infantry Rifles

35 units Line Infantry

5 units Foot Guards

4 units Engineers*

4 units Light Cavalry

5 units Heavy Cavalry

2 units Guard Cavalry

2 units Horse Artillery

4 units 8-pound Field Artillery

1 unit 12-pound Field Artillery

2 units 6-inch Howitzer

2 units Rocket Corps

1 Surgeon

1 Field Commander

Field Defensive Division:

4 units Light Infantry

1 unit Light Infantry Rifles

40 units Line Infantry

6 units Foot Guard

6 units Engineers*

4 units Heavy Cavalry

1 unit Guard Cavalry

5 units 8-pound Field Artillery

1 unit 12 pound Field Artillery

2 units 6-inch Howitzer

1 Surgeon

1 Field Commander

Bastion Defense Division:

6 units Light Infantry

40 units Line Infantry

6 units Foot Guard

6 units Engineers*

5 units 8-pound Field Artillery

2 units 12-pound Field Artillery

3 units 6-inch Howitzer

1 Surgeon

1 Field Commander

The above Divisions are balanced as closely as possible on a 'points' basis. Theoretically these divisions would fight to a standstill if all other considerations, such as the players' skill, the terrain and luck with the dice are equal. It can be easily seen that their applications range from hit-and-run to stonewall defence.

By designating composition in units it is possible for players to use squads, companies or regiments as the basic unit for tactical purposes. Most prefer to use the 10 man company as the smallest tactically operational unit.

For persons preferring to think in national types, the following tables are given. These divisional types do not parallel exactly the makeup of any European army of the period but again are of 'balanced inequality'. There were many revisions made in army organisations during this period; to meet the French successes, every army in Europe made at least one major revision between the years 1803-1815.

French:

- 7 units Light Infantry
- 6 units Line Grenadiers
- 8 units Line Infantry Fusiliers
- 10 units Line Infantry Voltigeurs
- 3 units Foot Guards
- 3 units Engineers*
- 3 units Light Cavalry
- 2 units Heavy Cavalry
- 2 units Lancer Cavalry
- 1 unit Guard Cavalry
- 1 unit 12-pound Field Artillery
- 2 units 8-pound Field Artillery
- 1 unit 6-inch Howitzer
- 3 units Horse Artillery
- 1 Surgeon
- 1 Field Commander

Austrian

- 5 units Light Infantry
- 4 units Line Grenadiers
- 24 units Musketeers
- 1 unit Foot Guard
- 2 units Engineers*
- 2 units Light Cavalry
- 2 units Heavy Cavalry
- 1 unit Lancer Cavalry
- 1 unit Guard Cavalry
- 1 unit 12-pound Field Artillery
- 2 units 8-pound Field Artillery

2 units Horse Artillery

1 unit 6-inch Howitzer

1 Surgeon

1 Field Commander

Prussian:

4 units Light Infantry

6 units Line Grenadiers

12 units Musketeers

8 units Landwehr

2 units Foot Guards

2 units Engineers*

1 unit Light Cavalry

2 units Heavy Cavalry

1 unit Lancer Cavalry

1 unit Guard Cavalry

1 unit 12-pound Field Artillery

2 units 8-pound Field Artillery

4 units Horse Artillery

2 units 6-inch Howitzer

1 Surgeon

1 Field Commander

British:

6 units Light Infantry

2 units Light Infantry Rifles

4 units Line Grenadiers

16 units Line Infantry

2 units Foot Guards

2 units Engineers*

2 units Light Cavalry

2 units Heavy Cavalry

1 unit Guard Cavalry

4 units 8-pound Field Artillery

2 units Horse Artillery

2 units 6-inch Howitzer

3 units Rocket Corps

1 Surgeon

1 Field Commander

Russian:

4 units Light Infantry

3 units Line Grenadiers

25 units Musketeers

1 unit Foot Guards

2 units Engineers*

2 units Heavy Cavalry

4 units Cossacks

2 units Guard Cavalry

1 unit 12-pound Field Artillery

2 units 8-pound Field Artillery

1 unit Horse Artillery

1 Surgeon

1 Field Commander

*Engineer units are usually considered optional units until one's forces number at least 300 infantry for each player. Supply troops are not mentioned, as they also optional units until the combatants are of sizeable quantities.

When your forces permit, you may wish to use the tables below:

Squad	8 men
Company	24 men - 3 squads plus optional Officer, Colour bearer, Drummer
Battalion	48 men - 2 companies plus officers, etc.
Regiment	96 men – 2 battalions
Brigade	288 men - 3 regiments
Corps	576 men - 2 brigades
Army	1728 men- 3 corps

Playing Surface

The first requirement (assuming an opponent) is a playing surface. Many persons prefer a sandtable. My preference is a six by twelve foot solid surface with variable terrain.

Terrain

The landscape on which the soldiers fight, is provided by model scenery laid upon the surface in such a manner to parallel the physical situation of an historic battlefield or an imaginative hypothetical topography.

Elevations

Varied elevation is accomplished by the use of one-half inch thick free-form contour sections stacked upon each other to form heights.

Any piece may move uphill provided an avenue exists up the elevation. Elevations having no 'steps' upwards are considered cliffs. A piece must be able to rest on each upward level for the height to be passable; where moving trays are used the players should agree which hills are passable, rather than attempting to balance trays on single contour projections. Light Infantry skirmishers, Rocket Corps and Scout Cavalry may be permitted to scale a height if one-half their base will fit the step; naturally these troops would find it difficult to fight while hanging by one hand!

Each piece climbing or descending hills will receive a penalty or augmentation of the move distance representing natural slowing down or speeding up of movement. The forfeiture or gain is always made to the leading man of each unit, the rest following accordingly.

Roads

Roads permit faster movement. Specific increments are given on page -
-. Roads should be described according to types and the frontage
capacity of each type agreed upon before beginning play. A Pike or High
road may allow a column of four to pass an artillery battery without
impeding the progress of either; a Wagon Trail may force a double-file
troop movement.

Rivers, Bridges and Fords

Streams may be crossed either by using bridges or designated fords.
Bridges will allow the same frontage as the road they serve and will not
impede progress unless damaged. Fords may be of varying widths and
will always exact a forfeit in moving distance.

Swampy, Sandy, or Soft Earth

Swampy, Sandy or ploughed ground will slow the progress of all units
and may prohibit the passage of ordnance or cavalry. It is usual to
designate a path through swamps, the frontage necessary to negotiate,
and units allowed. Artillery, except rockets, is not able to fire while
passing through swamps since recoil would bog the gun down.

Sandy soil and ploughed fields will slow movement but not so much
as marshes. It is recommended the forfeiture be decided before choosing
entry sides.

Normally the mapmaker will note frontage, forfeiture, etc. on the
map. A word of caution which shouldn't be necessary; if you continually
attempt to penalise opponents with unduly difficult terrain, you'd better
learn to play solo as you won't have many willing opponents!

Rocks, Trees and Buildings

Rocks, trees and buildings of various kinds are integrated into the
landscape to provide realism and furnish strategic points.

Terrain Maps

This game, being of simultaneous action, requires a map for each player
which should be prepared accurately and in reasonable detail. The scale
of 1 inch on the map to 1-1/2 feet of playing surface has been found quite
satisfactory.

The player issuing the challenge has the responsibility of preparing
the maps and playing surface. In cases of 'international war' the
defending player makes these preparations.

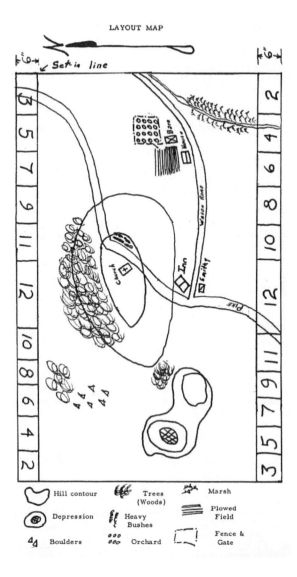

Entry Side

Only in cases of 'international war' where the invading army has approached on a predetermined route will a pre-decided entry route exist. In all other cases the entry side will be determined prior to beginning troop layout by the players throwing dice, the higher scoring player having his choice. This is another reason for maps being made available to players as early as possible.

Except for an assault in 'international war', each player must plan his initial layout and battle from two standpoints: it may well be that if A's forces are to enter from the South they must play a defensive role considering the terrain and forces on hand, whereas entry from the North may compel a policy of continual offense.

In preparing the terrain it is recommended that neither side be overwhelmingly favourable and that terrain advantages are balanced, even when an assault on established territory is underway.

Map Marking Symbols

The following symbols are used to indicate various units and formations when marking one's moves.

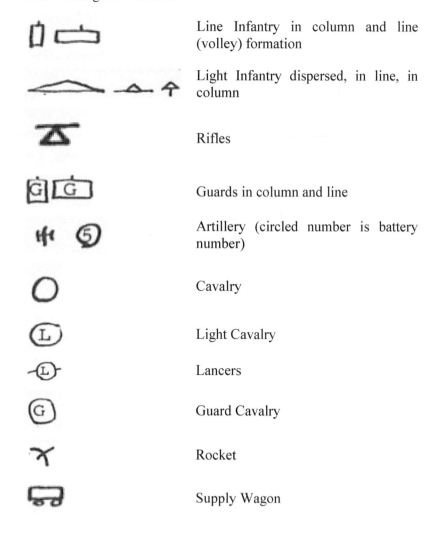

Line Infantry in column and line (volley) formation

Light Infantry dispersed, in line, in column

Rifles

Guards in column and line

Artillery (circled number is battery number)

Cavalry

Light Cavalry

Lancers

Guard Cavalry

Rocket

Supply Wagon

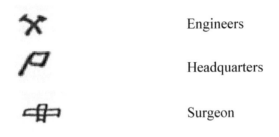

Engineers

Headquarters

Surgeon

It is mandatory that troops be set out in groups of like types to enter the field i.e., all rifle troops together, cavalry of one type, engineers, etc. Artillery may be dispersed as the Commander desires.

Bear in mind it is mandatory to show EACH UNIT for EACH MOVE of a game so long as that unit exists. Units not shown, or their intentions not marked clearly may NOT participate and, if attacked, are forced to withdraw without retaliating!

To indicate movement draw the appropriate unit symbol with an arrow indicating direction and the unit at its approximate position on the map at the end of the move as sketched above.

To indicate 'Charge', draw a broad arrow showing the unit, its route and the intended target:

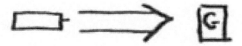

To indicate artillery fire, mark an 'F' by the battery's symbol:

Clear acetate surfaces placed over the maps make excellent plotting surfaces. The acetate may be cleaned with a damp cloth. Ordinary grease pencils serve to mark each move[1].

---

[1] Or one may use washable pens for use with overhead projectors or dry-wipe marker pens as used on whiteboards.

Photo 1 Russian Line Infantry in Volley Formation

Movement Tables

Infantry

Type	Line	Line Charge	Column	Road Column	Charge Column	Hill forfeit or gain per contour
Line	3"	5"	6"	9"	9"	1"
Guard	6"	9"	!2"	12"	12"	1"-2"
Lights	9" when dispersed as skirmishers. Skirmishers are free of Field Regulations		12"	12"	12"	1"

Cavalry

Type	Overland	Road	Charge	Hill forfeit or gain
Heavy	12"	18"	18"	1"-2"
Light	18"	24"	24"	1"-2"

The standard Cavalry formation 'at the trot' is: *guidon*, two ranks of two behind. Cavalry charges in a line abreast, each trooper no more than 1" from the nearest man of his troop. Light Cavalry, when dispersed as scouts, may form 'skirmish lines' with troopers 6" from the nearest man.

Ordnance

Two Horses

Type	Overland	Road	Hill loss/gain
Field	3"	6"	2"-1"
Siege	0	3"	2"-1"
Horse	9"	12"	1"-2"
Wagons	6"	9"	2"-1"

Four Horses

Type	Overland	Road	Hill loss/gain
Field	6"	9"	1"-1"
Siege	3"	6"	1"-1"
Horse	12"	18"	1"-2"
Wagons	9"	12"	1"-1"

Rockets have one pack horse; move 6" overland, 9" on roads; may be hand-carried 1" for each man in crew if horse is killed, maximum 3"; forfeit and gain 1" for hills.

Measurement

In measuring movement, firing range or melee involvement, the measurement is made from the base of the individual figures or from the centre of the front moving stand. The only exception is a situation where an encounter takes place between two groups of men – in this case a necessity for a 'grace area' exists. In explanation, suppose eight men were firing upon twenty; If those receiving fire were in double-ranked formation with one of the rear rank just slightly out of range it would be false to consider the rear troops as not being liable to injury; by the same token if a portion of a group of men is involved by proximity in a melee, the entire group is involved, since it is false to assume that only a portion of a company would become embroiled in hand-to-hand fighting. The grace area is intended to deal with these circumstances.

When measuring artillery or supply wagon movement the axle (front axle on wagons) is the point of measurement. The centre of the launcher is the point used for measuring Rocket movement.

Personnel Classifications

Before going further, here is a table of personnel classifications in use during the time period by various countries. The 'Elite' of each category is named first. Bear in mind these are the basic unit types for game purposes.

Light Infantry

FRENCH	AUSTRIAN	PRUSSIAN	RUSSIAN	BRITISH
Carabinier	Jaeger (Tyrol)	Jaeger	Yeager	Lt. Rifles
Lt. Voltigeur	Lt. Infantry	-----	-----	Lt. Infantry
Chasseur a Pied	------	------	------	

Line Infantry

FRENCH	AUSTRIAN	PRUSSIAN	RUSSIAN	BRITISH
Guard	Guard	Guard	Guard	Guard
Grenadier	Grenadier	Grenadier	Grenadier	Grenadier
Fusiliers	Musketeers	Musketeers	Musketeers	Regulars
Voltiguer	----	----	-----	Lt. Co.
----	----	-----	-----	Fusilier

Cavalry

FRENCH	AUSTRIAN	PRUSSIAN	RUSSIAN	BRITISH
Guard	Guard	Guard	Guard	Life Guards
Dragoon	Dragoon	Dragoon	Dragoon	Dragoon
Hussar	Hussar	Hussar	----	Light Dragoon
Lancer	Uhlan	Uhlan	Cossack	-----

In actuality, Guards were usually referred to as Grenadiers, but in our game we have two classifications with 'Grenadiers' being the elite of the Line. Within the Guard classification (especially for the French) was found every unit type within the army's makeup; Napoleon's Imperial Guard was a complete army within the army, which other nations never equalled. In attempting to construct a game as broad as this it is nearly impossible to take into account the entire structure of all armies so the above classifications were chosen. Knowledgeable persons with specific units will know where to assign them in the morale and ability categories. There are many excellent sources for those wishing more information which will be found in the suppliers section.

Field Regulations

In the period with which we are concerned, waging war depended on well-trained and disciplined troops. To draw up in lines abreast, fire muskets, then either advance with bayonet and sabre or stand and reload while other ranks fire demanded the ultimate in discipline and loyalty. Our modern day soldiers still perform many of those movements on the parade ground, but never in battle.

Skirmisher tactics used by American Indians and Colonials brought about the end of a 'classic' style of warfare that, in its basics, had existed since the late seventeenth century.

Troops in our 'Little Wars' will march and manoeuvre under the following limitations and orders, hereafter referred to as Field Regulations.

Troops march to the scene of conflict either in line or column; line is defined as more men along the unit's front than behind the leaders. So, two lines of ten men abreast constitutes a line for movement; two lines of ten men one behind the other constitutes a column for movement.

Troops change from one formation to another by <u>facing</u> or by <u>moving.</u>

Commanders must imagine themselves giving specific orders to their men, indeed, some will find themselves shouting commands, then reaching out to execute them, shifting troops by hand. The more sophisticated will issue commands under their breaths, but they *will* issue them!

On a single turn, troops may perform any <u>two</u> of <u>three</u> possibilities:

<u>Face and Move, Face and Fire, Move and Fire</u>. They may not move, then face, then fire or any combination of three ordered movements on

one turn. Should they be in contact at the end of the move, the troops enter into hand-to-hand combat (melee).

Troops will march in proper order. If a change in direction is desired it will be executed by the 'Flank' command (which would constitute active facing) or by the 'Column' command. If a contingent of troops in one formation is to change formation while en route (i.e. from column to line while maintaining the direction of the march), it is recommended that, when going into line, the forward element stop and those behind move up alongside. If changing from line to column, it is recommended the leading elements move the normal distance and others fall in behind.

Move Tray: although there is a certain satisfying thrill in moving individual men, when one has over 200 pieces to move it gets tedious and time-consuming. The use of moving trays has become universal.

Skirmisher Trays: Light Infantry are mounted on four-man trays as in photo 12

Squad Trays: if one's basic unit is the squad of 5, the recommended tray is a piece of Bristol Board (or other light, strong wood) twice the width of the base of the men and of sufficient length to allow one-half base distance between men. With the men placed as in the sketch, they are moving in a linear front.

To indicate columnar movement, one may turn an end man to face the direction of march or turn the entire unit. Where the numbers of men permit using the company as the basic unit, allow a full base-width between the ranks and one-half base-width between files and the unit would be:

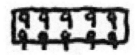

Again, to indicate columnar movement, the two men on the end would be faced or the entire unit faced in the direction of march. The ideal formation to the author is the regiment, using three trays.

In photos 2, 3 and 4, a 'route front change' occurs. The lead tray is the measuring point. At the beginning of the move, tray #1 remains stationary and the following trays come alongside each other to form the volley line in photo 4, at the end of the move.

Photos 2, 3 and 4 Prussians changing from Column to Line

Photo 3

If the unit was in line at the beginning of the move and wished to form a column, the reverse would hold true. The tray containing the colours would then move its full distance, the others following.

Men may be affixed to the trays by using children's modelling clay, a non-hardening mastic (Eberhard Faber makes one called 'Holdit' which is excellent), or any soft material. This allows casualties to be detached easily and, when trays are emptied, they may be taken from the table and filled with men 'killed' in action, which makes 'housecleaning' a little easier.

Photo 4

When one's army grows large enough to permit 24 man regiments, three 8 man trays are used in photos 2, 3 and 4.

When mounting the pieces on the trays, place the leading edge of the front rank bases as close to the leading edge of the stand as possible

Infantry Move Possibilities

In column at move beginning	In line at move beginning
Advance or Charge	Fire, Advance or Charge
Form line, move	Fire, Fall back (2" Line, 4" Guards)
Form line, Fire	Fire, Form column
Form line	Fire, Form column
Advance in column, form line	Form column
	Form column, Move
	Move in line, Form column
	Move in line, Fire.

The above Field Regulations must be adhered to by Line and Guard infantry at all times.

Light Infantry, Engineers, Supply, Staff and the Surgeon operate with freedom. Light Infantry may form into column for road movement or for charging, otherwise (unless mounted on move stands) Light Infantry may not be more than 2" from another man of the unit.

Stragglers

Line groups of less than five (5) men are considered stragglers and move at the fixed rate of three inches (3") per turn regardless of terrain. Such men are stragglers until they are attached to a unit - another like Infantry group, Artillery crew, or Supply wagon. Supply wagons may transport stragglers to another unit as passengers. If stragglers are attached to another Infantry unit of similar status they resume their previous situation; if attached to Field Artillery they will move with that unit as permitted, assuming its identity. Infantry may be attached to an Elite unit but not assume that unit's increased abilities; they may serve as the crew of a Horse Artillery unit but when the gun moves they move at the Field Artillery rate. When Infantry are assigned to Supply units for the purpose of being servers they assume that unit's foot move and are freed of Field Regulations.

Sequence of Game Actions

<u>All</u> actions occur simultaneously as in actual battles; this is not a 'move, counter-move' form of wargame. The sequence:

Mark Maps

Fire or move Artillery

Assess Artillery damage

Move Infantry, Engineers, Cavalry, etc.

Build works, bridges, etc.

Fire Volley and Skirmisher fire

Fight Melees

Mark Maps

gives a total of seven actions per move. Where an intended movement is in doubt, it is customary to allow the opponent to examine one's map.

During a turn a player may move <u>all</u> of his units, <u>some</u> of his units or <u>none</u> of his units – he may move or fire artillery, transport supplies, build fortifications (works), take prisoners, fire musketry or enter into hand-to-hand combat. In short, during a turn a player may utilise his troops as he wishes provided he stays within the rules/limitations ascribed to each unit.

Supply wagons speed ammunition to batteries, cavalry charges are launched, heights are taken and lost, men are killed and wounded, prisoners are taken and rescued; and victory may hinge upon a small contingent of hard-pressed but valiant troops. Thus is the game of war played. A number of various coloured dice, a fair amount of luck, a decent judgement of distance and a perceptive mind will decide the outcome of the affair.

Entry Methods

There are several methods of entry, each having its particular advantages. In each case, the players mark their initial layout on the plotting surface over their maps. You will note in figure 1, we recommend a set-in line six inches from the edges of the table, this is to allow as many troops as possible to be placed on the field at the beginning of the game.

In all instances, the correct placement of troops must be noted by both Commanders. If there are units *en route* they must be noted on a slip of paper placed in an envelope before starting the game with the appropriate move marked on the envelope.

Map Layout

The 'standard' layout is to mark one's troops in their proper positions on the plotting surface of the maps. After both commanders have finished marking, the troops are then placed on the board to start the game.

Curtain Entry[2]

A variation of the map layout consists of drawing a curtain across the centre of the table and keeping it closed until all troops are in their starting positions. When the curtain is pulled, both generals usually have harsh things to say to themselves as they see the enemy forces placed entirely differently from where they guessed they would be!

Card Layout

The card layout assumes that the range of the commanders' eyesight is somewhat less than the distance across the playing surface, which may be somewhat more realistic. It is handled by using a number of file cards. On the underside of each card is made a diagram of the units it represents and the card travels across the playing surface at the rate of the slowest unit on the card. When within positive identification distance of enemy units (30" seems most agreeable) the card is turned over and the units are placed on the playing surface. A card may represent any unit from a Company to a Corps. Remember, the card must show all units represented and their overall formation. Here the map is marked

---

[2] This long-established method was proposed by HG Wells in *Little Wars*.

showing Unit #1, Unit#2, etc. until actual sighting then the normal marking is followed.

Random Entry

On sketch #1 you will notice each side of the table is marked in sections, 12 in the centre, the odd numbers on the left, even on the right. Each numbered section is one foot long, except the centre section which is two feet long. This, of course, assumes a twelve foot table.

In random entry, comparable to a 'pickup' game of ball, the procedure followed is for the commanders to alternate choosing a unit to place on the table, throwing two dice, and placing the unit in the area indicated by the total score, then marking the plotting surface. You may wind up with a very disorganised entry, but a very interesting game!

Simultaneity of Actions

There may be many instances where simultaneous volleys will be exchanged by infantry formations or simultaneous cannonades occur in counter-battery fire.

In these instances, each volley is computed using the number of men participating that made up the unit at the beginning of the turn; only after *both* volleys have been fired are casualties removed from the units.

In cases of counter-battery fire, if the first gun firing scores a hit, the target is allowed to fire and then is turned on its side if damaged, or removed if destroyed, according to the damage tables as given on page --.

In other words, simultaneous action means just that: each party is allowed to fire artillery, volleys and skirmishers and then casualties are removed.

Troops charging into hand-to-hand combat will suffer losses from musketry, then close in melee.

Photo 5 French Imperial Guard Artillery

Artillery

Wargame Artillery is either overwhelmingly powerful or uselessly ineffectual! We have striven to achieve a balance which parallels the actual Artillery usage in the Napoleonic period.

Field Artillery has been standardised as 4 pound Horse and Field, 8 and 12 pound Field; 6 inch Field Howitzers and Rockets. 24 pound siege guns were used but seldom in open field battles.

Rockets were becoming part of field ordnance. True, rockets did not inflict the damage of present day fire but they could be effective. Rockets played decisive parts in the battles of Boulogne (18066), Copenhagen (1807), Walcheren (1807), Adour (1813), Leipzig (1813) and also at Bladensburg (1814) on the North American continent during the War of 1812[3].

Rockets of the period had explosive heads and impact fuses. Although they were fired at troops (recruits would often break under heavy concentration) their main targets were Artillery and Supply points with incendiary intent.

The first physical action of each turn is to move or fire Artillery according to the following table of possible actions:

Move

Unlimber

Load

Fire

Limber

When measuring Artillery movement, use the axle of the guns as the measuring point. For Rocket, use the centre of the launcher.

Howitzers operate a Field Artillery except they are not issued solid-round shot; 4, 8, 12 and 24 pounders are issued no explosive shells.

---

[3] And feature in *The Star Spangled Banner*: 'The rockets' red glare, bombs bursting in air'

Limber Chest Capacity

(for game purposes):

TYPE	CLASS	ROUNDS	CANISTER	MINIMUM CREW TO FIRE	ACTIONS PER TURN
4-pound	Horse	15	5	3	5
8-pound	Field	15	5	3	4
12-pound	Field	10	3	3	4
24-pound	Siege	8	3	5	3
6" Howitzer	Field	10*	5	3	4
Rocket	Field	40*	0	1	6+

*Explosives

+The possible actions for a Rocket crew are:

Move

Unpack

Load (5 rockets)

Fire (5 rockets)

Pack

To keep an ammunition inventory, the batteries are numbered, and this number is shown on the plotting surface. A corresponding inventory sheet can be made from 3" x 5" file cards. The round is always marked off before measurement and windage calculations.

Where supply wagons are used, or in games involving supply points, artillery may receive additional ammunition via the wagons. For further information see the section on Special Services.

Solid roundshot bounces along the ground, skipping over men in some instances and bowling over in others. It varies in range and destructive effect against various objects according to the table below. Three 'damages' constitute one 'destruct'. Damage 'points' are cumulative from guns of various calibres.

An object hit in the red section of the trajectory stick, including a hit which causes a ricochet, constitutes an automatic damage point; if hit in the green section, throw one die, if the score is 5 or 6, a damage point is allowed, otherwise there is no damage.

With the exception of works, all the below are destroyed by a single Howitzer shell if the object is wholly within the burst circle. If less than all is in the burst circle, throw one die: scores of 4 or below damage the target, 5 or 6 destroy it.

Not more than 3 inches of works may be destroyed by a Howitzer shell and then only if a 5 or 6 is scored on the die, whether or not the entire section of works is within the burst circle.

Target Destruction Table

Targets are destroyed according to the following scale:

Target	Ordnance Class Firing				
	Rocket	4#	8#	12#	24#
Rocket Launcher	1/3	1/3	1/3	1/3	1/3
Supply Wagon	1/3	2/3	1/3	1/3	1/3
1" section wood fence	1/3	1/3	1/3	1/3	1/3
1" section stone wall	1	2/3	1/3	1/3	1/3
1" section wood bridge	2/3	2/3	1/3	1/3	1/3
1 wall wood building	2/3	2/3	2/3	1/3	1/3
Artillery Piece	1/3	1	1	2/3	1/3
1" section stone bridge	1	1	2/3	2/3	1/3
1 wall stone building	1	1	2/3	2/3	1/3
1" section works	1-2/3	1-1/3	1	1	2/3

Trees, bushes and other growth are knocked down by roundshot or destroyed by shells or rockets. Roundshot will destroy (going up in poundage) 1, 3, 5 and 10 trees in the red sections. Howitzers destroy all trees in a burst circle; rockets the first tree hit.

Works are earthen breastworks built by Engineers and were so impervious to cannonades that they were often more desirable than stone fort walls. When Fort Sumter was bombarded the defenders built works from the rubble and considered themselves better protected than before!

The sketches below are trajectory sticks for 4, 8, 12 and 24 pound guns. Men in the white sections are safe, the ball flew over them - or they ducked quickly; men in the red sections which were touched by the stick are killed; those touched by the stick in the green section are wounded (ball rolling along ground breaking shins, etc.). The yellow section next to the muzzle is the 'muzzle blast' and all men in that area are wounded. Any piece may elect to fire a 'short charge' and will use the trajectory for a lesser rated gun. The trajectory stick is placed with the yellow section touching the muzzle so it extends toward the intended target. Guns on elevations gain one inch range for each contour which is added to the green area. Howitzers and Rockets do not use the trajectory patterns nor do they gain for elevation since their fire is always high arc.

In the initial white area of the trajectory stick, and six inches from the muzzle, guns may fire over the following heights: 4#- 2 contours, 8#- 4 contours, 12#- 6 contours, 24#- 8 contours. Howitzers and Rockets may fire over any height from the muzzle or launcher.

Trajectory Sticks

Normal elevation trajectory sticks

Sketch #2

Photos 6 & 7: French Horse Artillery

Depressed muzzle trajectory sticks

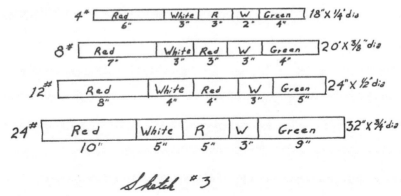

Sketch #3

The 'depressed muzzle' trajectory stick is designed for level ground. Since it is impossible to account and adjust for all the possible ramifications and situations which will arise in wargames, a blanket ruling states Artillery cannot be sufficiently depressed to hit a target less than man-height within 3" if sitting at the edge of a contour, add 2" for each contour. If solid-round hits an ascending contour in the red sections of flight, it stops.

Any projectile which hits water, swampy ground, sandy soil or ploughed ground stops upon impact.

Since no Artillery crew hits the target every time (not even today with electronic rangefinders!) we allow for windage. The Windage Calculator is a four-inch long stick marked at one-inch intervals:

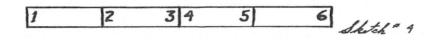

Sketch #4

Windage Calculator

Place the proper trajectory stick with the green section at the intended target. Place the Windage Calculator, 1" to the gun's left, at the beginning of the second white section of the trajectory stick with the trajectory stick crossing the 3-4 centre line. Throw one die, then move the trajectory stick until it crosses the mark indicated by the die score. A 3 or 4 indicates a hit (or at least the round went in the intended direction), other numbers place the round off to the right or left. On guns with longer ranges, it becomes more difficult to get a near-miss but the percentage of probability (33-1/3%) remains the same.

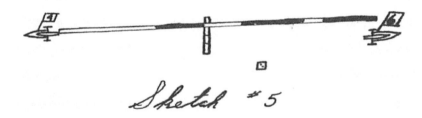

Sketch #5

In sketch #5, battery #4 has fired at enemy battery #6. The Windage die scores 2, so the round flies off target to the left.

Howitzer Firing

Howitzers have a maximum range of 36" and a minimum of 6", at closer range they fired Canister or limbered up and retired! The range must be estimated and given in even inches, the round marked off the battery's inventory and then:

1. With a yardstick, measure from the muzzle of the gun to the target, place the Windage Calculator one-half the given range and throw one die, then proceed as above.
2. Place a 4" diameter 'burst circle' with the end of the <u>actual</u> flight path (as affected by Windage) in the centre; for each man or horse completely within the circle, or whose major portion is within the circle, throw one die and assess injuries according to the following:

> 1 Unharmed
>
> 2-3-4 Wounded
>
> 5-6 Killed

Rockets

Rockets, basically a British weapon, did not come into full use on the continent until around 1812-13 (authorities disagree) but were used rather extensively by ships to bombard targets on shore before this time.

Rockets in use on land were the Congreve type, launched from a trough-like platform and at best, somewhat erratic on windy days.

The maximum range for Rockets is 30 inches. The range must be estimated and given, the round marked off the battery's inventory and for each rocket launched throw one die to determine its fate:

1   Rocket explodes on launcher, launcher destroyed, crew injured

2-3   Rocket launches, wind catches it one-half distance, throws rocket off 90 degrees (2, right, 3, left) for remainder of run

4-5-6   Rocket launches normally, affected only by normal windage

To determine normal windage, use the same procedure as outlined for Howitzers.

Personnel are injured within a 1-1/2" diameter 'burst circle' according to the following scale:

1-2-3   Unharmed

4-5   Wounded

6   Killed

Rockets passing directly over troops (other than foot or horse Guardsmen) cause a morale check to be made.

If one is inclined to doubt the rocket's ability to destroy an Artillery piece with one direct hit, consider this: an Artillery limber may have five hundred pounds or more of unstable blackpowder, so a rocket hitting it would have the same effect as dropping a lighted paper match in a petrol tank!

Canister

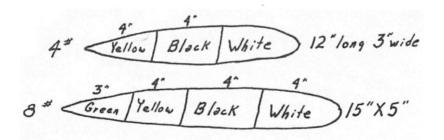

Canister patterns may be made out of wire coat hangers, pieces of strip metal or other material. The width should be arrived at not more than ¼

the total distance from the muzzle and remain at maximum width to ¼ the distance from the end of the pattern. Cross-pieces may be held in place by metal epoxy glue or solder, and may be painted the colour of the next succeeding segment.

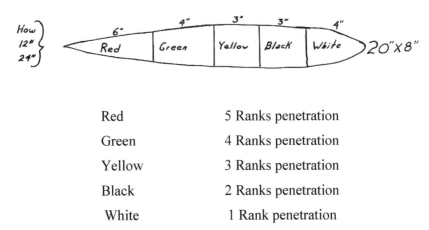

Red	5 Ranks penetration
Green	4 Ranks penetration
Yellow	3 Ranks penetration
Black	2 Ranks penetration
White	1 Rank penetration

Obviously the Horse guns were least effective. When the charge has penetrated the maximum number of ranks permitted by the colour coding, ranks behind, although still in the pattern, are unharmed.

To determine casualties cast one die for each man or horse within the pattern:

1 - 2 Unharmed

3-4-5 Wounded

6 Killed

Obviously, canister fired at a slight Enfilade angle will expose larger numbers of troops to injury.

Damaged Ordnance

Damaged ordnance is unusable until repaired and may be hand-dragged 1" providing there is a complete crew with the gun. The piece of ordnance may be repaired by remaining inoperative for two full turns with a minimum crew, or the proper number of 'detailed' infantrymen with one regular Artillerist to supervise. Three consecutive damages without intervening repair destroy the piece.

Ricochet

Solid roundshot will ricochet when it strikes a substantial object such as boulders or stone walls at an angle. After striking it then continues on the new course of flight for one-half the balance of its normal range. Men struck on the ricochet course are liable to wounds or death, just as on the original course. Ricochet firing was useful since, according to one authority, gunners would fire so that the ball would just clear a defensive wall, would bounce around among the enemy guns, wound the crews and break the gun carriages.

In computing the ricochet, the angle of reflection (new course) is equal to the angle of incidence.

Rockets and Howitzer shells explode upon hitting a solid object rather than ricocheting.

Photo 8: Prussian Infantry in Line

Infantry

Infantry's job in wargaming is the same as it always has been in actual war: to close with the enemy and defeat them with musketry, bayonet, rifle butt or fists. The fighting values of various infantry are given in the section on Combat Actions.

As noted in the Field Regulations, Line and Guard infantry follow definite manoeuvres and formational rules in the field. Light infantry have considerable freedom but, in some ways, are less valuable.

Light Infantry

The basic assignment of Light Infantry is to screen the larger concentrations, acting as a 'buffer' and harass the enemy with skirmisher firing. Light infantry may also form and deliver volleys. Light infantry will seldom launch a charge into enemy formations, this is not their forte.

When not dispersed as skirmishers (and not mounted on four-man stands), we allow lights to operate with 3" between men in a unit. If the unit is to be assembled in column or volley formation one move is required to bring the dispersed group together, on the following turn they perform whatever function desired. Light infantry may be assigned as Artillery or Supply replacements.

Instead of bayonets and sabres, lights were generally armed with carbines and the short 'musician's' sword. Rifles in use were allocated to the light infantry troops. In our time period, the British were the only European army using rifles to any extent. For game purposes, we allow a certain percentage of rifles for all hypothetical divisions listed on pages 5 and 6.

Line Infantry

Line Infantry is the backbone of the army. Line elites are Grenadiers as distinguished from Foot Guards.

Line infantry performs as outlined in the Field Regulations. Line fires volleys, charges into melee, acts in every respect as did the fighting men of Napoleonic times.

Except for stragglers, line infantrymen always fire volley. Stragglers, by definition, are groups of Line Infantry other than Guards, of less than five men.

Line infantrymen may be assigned to act as artillery servers to fill out a crew but must have a regular Artillerist with them to fire the gun. Whenever line infantry is detached for this purpose, or to act as Supply Wagon drivers, a full squad must be assigned although this may be parcelled among several guns or wagons.

Stragglers

Line survivors of an action numbering less than five men are stragglers until attached to another unit. If a lesser-rated infantry man is attached to higher-rated unit, he takes on that unit's move distance (except mounted units) but not their special offensive or defensive characteristics. Line infantry men may be attached to Guard units but do not assume their special abilities, including forced marches. If line stragglers are assigned to Horse Artillery as replacements, they may only move 6" per turn.

Naturally, the infantrymen of any status may not be assigned to Cavalry as replacements!

Stragglers, until attached, may not launch an offensive action. They may defend themselves if attacked by firing skirmisher fire or retaliating to hand-to-hand attacks.

Guards

In our game, Guards are the elite. In Napoleon's army, the Guards were of every classification from Chasseur to Grenadier a Cheval and the hobbyist with sufficient pieces may wish to operate with this assuming he compensates for the larger number of elites by allowing larger numbers of line for his opponents.

Guardsmen, because of superior experience, training and equipment are given special status when fighting hand-to-hand. Their musketry is the same as other line infantry; it is in hand-to-hand fighting and mobility that the guard excels the rest of the line infantry.

Infantry Square

The square was an almost impregnable formation, moving slowly across the field. Nothing could launch a frontal assault with any certainty of success on an unbroken side except for Lancer cavalry.

To be effective, the square must have a complete unit (Squad, Company or Regiment) to a side. The square moves at a crawl (remember only ¼ of the men are moving forward, ½ are moving sideways, and ¼ are moving backwards) and in our game has a move of 2" and may only move across open ground. Even Guards in a square cannot extend this move distance.

An extended move is allowed to form a Square and the mechanics are:

The Square is indicated on the plotting surface with one unit designated as the 'front'. The 'front' unit remains stationary (unless necessary to go into line formation) and three other units may then move a maximum of 10" to form the square. On the next move the square is stationary, this turn is necessary for 'final forming and resting'. On the second turn, the square may begin its advance.

Any side of the square may lose volleys independent of the other sides.

On the initial die throw in hand-to-hand combat, an unbroken side of the square receives an additional Evaluation Point on each die for their formation making the Square a Superior Position, which it definitely is!

Once a side of a Square is broken by any means whatever (musketry, artillery fire, Lancers or hand-to-hand fighting) that side may be charged by any cavalry unit. If a unit (foot or horse) succeeds in breaking a side of a square other units in the square are subject to Enfilade attack!

Photo 9: Prussian Infantry Square

Photo 10: French Dragoons and Mamelukes du Garde

Cavalry

Cavalry's duty is to perform the charge. Except for Dragoons and Mamelukes, cavalrymen fight with sabres or lances while mounted.

The two Cavalry speeds are the 'Trot' and 'Charge'. At the trot all units except Light Cavalry move in a body of guidon, two ranks of two behind. Scouts may disperse with not more than 5" between men of the same unit.

If one mounts cavalry on move stands there are several variations that fit game purposes: Light Cavalry mounted four abreast on 'Skirmish' stands as in photo #11; the 1-2-2 formation; 2-3 formation; or 5 abreast.

Photo 11: French Dragoons

Dragoons:

Dragoons are permitted to fire skirmisher fire while mounted at musket range. Dragoons may dismount to act as skirmishers or to form volley lines but one horse-holder is required for every four men afoot. Dismounted Dragoons may not operate further than 12" from their mounts. If dismounted Dragoons are involved in hand-to-hand combat they have the same value as foot Light Infantry. While dismounted, Dragoons have a 9" move.

On a single turn, Dragoons may move within the limits of their allowable normal distance, dismount and fire but not remount.

Lancers:

The only Cavalry unit allowed to charge an unbroken Infantry Square is the Lancer. The reach of lances (variously 12 to 18 feet) outreached infantrymen with fixed bayonets.

Lancers receive an extra green die on the initial cast when they charge into hand-to-hand combat. If Lancers attack at Enfilade, they receive the normal extra red die plus their extra green die on the initial cast.

Mamelukes

Mamelukes were attached to the French Guard Cavalry. These sons of the desert went into battle with a mace, a morning star, a musketoon, some other weapons included a blunderbuss, at least two and sometimes four hand guns, a scimitar, and at least two daggers or short swords! These men were intensely loyal to Napoleon and fought with fanatical fury, for this reason we also allow them an extra Green die on their initial cast when they charge into hand-to-hand combat.

The Charge

Unless charging, Cavalry is useless. If attacked while sitting, they are handicapped by nervous horses and thus fight on an even footing with line infantrymen.

All Cavalry accept the forfeits when attacking a Superior Position.

Cavalry charges in line abreast. To successfully execute the charge at least one man must be in contact with the enemy at the end of the move distance. Cavalry charges by definition are Assault Melees and are resolved as such.

Like all units, cavalry will have to accept a volley from the enemy if a morale check of the enemy unit permits. Horses, being somewhat smarter than some men, cavalry may swerve under the force of a full volley and when this occurs the direction of the swerve will be given by the dice in the following manner:

The breakaway or swerve is assumed to have happened within volley range of the charged unit. The breakaway happens when the cavalry unit's morale check in the face of a full volley calls for other than pressing home a charge.

Cast one die:

1-2 Swerve to the right the number of move distances indicated by Morale table.

3-4 Swerve to the left the number of move distances indicated by Morale table.

5-6 Retire directly to rear as indicated by Morale table.

Units swerving are liable to receive musketry from other enemy units in volley formation - at Enfilade!

When cavalry breaks from a volley, one-half the 'swerve' (fall back) distance will be parallel to the charged unit(s), then the cavalry will turn out of musket range and continue.

BREAKTHROUGH

Cavalry may accomplish a 'Breakthrough' if they indicate the desired path and annihilate the unit(s) interposed between their starting position and the extent of their possible move. Unit, by this definition, implies the whole entity of some kind, so that should they attack a line comprised of 4 regiments, for example, they must remove the whole of one regiment in order to breakthrough. In another instance, they may charge a line of 2 regiments and a battalion; should the charge be launched at the battalion, they must destroy this unit.

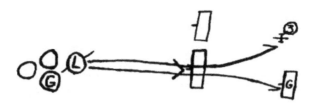

The desired path is indicated on the map; player A indicates a charge at regiment #1 of B's army, then continue into regiment #2. Thus beginning another melee, or he might indicate that he will turn to either side following breakthrough. Enfilade will NOT occur during the second phase of this turn unless breaking through one side of an Infantry Square. By the same token, the second unit charged would NOT issue a volley!

Cavalry Horses as Teams

Cavalry horses may be used to pull Artillery or Wagons to replace killed or wounded teams. However, since these horses are not trained for draft work, progress is slowed 2" per turn for an equal number of horses.

Combat Actions

Combat actions are decided by the throw of the dice interpreted by a number of simple rules.

There are two classes of combat actions: Firing and Melee. Firing is defined as the action of men delivering musketry at their adversaries. It is initiated by one group at another group and involves only those delivering the fire. Only one shot per man is delivered per turn.

Firing

Firing is subdivided into two types: Skirmisher Fire and Volley Fire. All troops with the exception of Light Infantry Rifle regiments are equipped with muskets. Skirmisher fire is delivered by Light Infantry, special services (Artillerists, Engineers, Supply), mounted Cavalry and (for defensive purposes only) stragglers. Skirmisher fire is defined as: fire delivered by an individual at a specifically chosen target. Light Infantrymen acting in this capacity could be termed 'sharpshooters'.

Musket range is 9", rifle range 12"

Photo 12: French Voltigeurs skirmishing against Prussian Landwehr

Skirmisher Fire Effect

Effect is calculated for each man firing by casting two dice; if the total is less than 6, it is a miss; 6 through 9 is a wound; 10 through 12 is a kill. This scale changes when firing into Superior Position. Consult the table for Skirmisher Fire into Superior Position for the altered scales.

In photo #12, French Voltigeurs face Prussian Line. The French Light Infantrymen are mounted on four man skirmisher stands. In this instance, the French have the choice of firing volley or skirmisher fire while the Prussians must fire volley.

Volley Fire Effect

Volley fire may be delivered by any unit except mounted Cavalry, formed into volley order in single or double lines facing the target. It is the only type of firing permitted Line Infantry. Volley fire is group firing at a general target. The basic is the unit's fire and is measured from the centre of the front line of the volley group. Providing the target is within the range, the effect is calculated by the cast of two dice - one Red, the other Green. The Green die represents wounds and is calculated first with its pips divided into the number issuing fire. It does not matter how many are being fired upon. The figure arrived at from the division of the Green die into the number firing gives the count of enemy troops wounded. Disregard fractions, there are no 'half-wounds'. The Red die represents kills and is calculated through the multiplication of its pips by the number issuing fire; this sum is then divided by the 10 points necessary to kill a man with musket fire. The total computation gives the count of enemy troops killed. Again, disregard fractional figures; there can be no 'half-kills'. Following are some examples of volley fire calculations:

Example A: Number issuing fire, 10. Green die scores 5, Red die 1.

Result: 2 wounds, 1 kill. 10 divided by 5 = 2 for the Green (wounds); 10 x 1 = 10 divided 10 = 1 for the Red (kills)

Example B: Number issuing fire, 20. Green die scores 5, Red die 1.

Result: 4 wounds, 2 kills. 20 divided by 5 = 4 for the Green (wounds), 20 x 1 = 20 divided by 10 = 2 for the Reds (kills)

Example C: Number issuing fire, 8. Green die scores 5, Red die 4.

Result 1 wound, 3 kills. 8 divided by 5 = 1 (disregard remainder 3) for the Green die (wounds); 8 x 4 = 32 divided 10 = 3 (disregard remainder 2) for the Red (kills)

It is <u>possible</u> for the number killed and wounded by a volley to be <u>greater</u> than the number issuing fire – the only action where this is permitted!

Volley fire is also affected when directed against a Superior Position. Consult the table Volley Fire into a Superior Position to get its lessoned effectiveness.

In determining volley fire always calculate the effect of the green die first; the red die acts against the survivors.

Firing against Horse Troops

Where horses are in range of musketry fire, it is logical that some shots would hit the horses, leaving the men afoot (or ordnance short a horse) while the men remain unharmed. Again, one die is cast for the entire unit, even when skirmisher fire, and the following table is used:

Casualty Percentages

1	All horses
2-3-4	Half horses, half men
5-6	All men

Photo 13: Austrian Grenadiers and Musketeers charging Bavarians

Morale Table

There are four instances when a player is <u>forced</u> to check the morale of his troops: upon receiving a charge; charging into a full volley; when doubles are thrown in melee, and in determining the effectiveness of rocket fire.

Melee:

When double numbers are thrown in melee (actual, not using increment or evaluation) the player against whom the throw is made must check the morale of <u>all</u> troops engaged (including those engaged by proximity) after personnel damages for that throw have been exacted. Two dice are thrown and the troops react according to the following table:

Die Cast	Foot and Horse Guards, Staff Surgeon	Grenadiers, Cuirassiers, Hussars, Engineers	Artillery Light Infantry Other Cavalry	Line Infantry Supply Troops
7-12	Stay	Stay	Stay	Stay*
6	Stay	Stay	Stay	Wd.-1#
5	Stay	Stay	Wd.-1	Wd.-2
4	Stay	Wd.-1	Wd.-2	Wd.-3
3	Wd.-1	Wd.-2	Wd.-3	Diss.~
2	Wd.-2	Diss.	Diss.	Diss.

*Troops hold their ground, continue fighting, or press home charge.

Troops withdraw in good order, maintaining formation, specified number of move distances facing the enemy. Troops must accept an opposed throw (including increment) by the enemy, however the opposition merely limits the amount of damage inflicted, withdrawing troops may not exact damage. The same rules concern consecutive attacks as in cases of voluntary withdrawal. As in the case of voluntary withdrawal, if the attacker does not press his advantage and a turn intervenes without the withdrawn troops being attacked, they may initiate aggressive action against the forces that caused withdrawal or any other enemy unit.

~ Troops flee in disorder 4 move distances, backs to enemy. One turn is required to re-form dissolved troops, during which time they may not move toward the enemy. If a unit dissolves and the opponent has Cavalry surviving the melee, it is assumed Cavalry pursued the dissolved units and chopped them to pieces - all are dead. If there is no enemy Cavalry, dissolving units must accept one unopposed melee cast (including increment).

Morale checks are made by Troop, Company, or Regimental units, Artillery batteries and Supply Wagons. A Grenadier or Guard unit will add one point to the die cast of lesser evaluated units immediately adjacent to it (on each side or behind). If the Guard or Grenadier Company falters, one point will be deducted from adjacent units.

A Staff Officer within one move of any unit will add one point to that unit's morale cast. If he or the Surgeon withdraws, deduct one point from Guards and Grenadiers, two points from all other units cast!

The morale of each unit passed by a withdrawing or dissolving unit must be checked since morale loss is contagious. Check morale starting with the point of contact and then going outward, checking units involved by proximity.

Troops withdrawing by any method must retire directly toward the unit's rear, not necessarily toward their rear area. True, this may put them in jeopardy of an Enfilade attack on the next turn. Morale against rocketry is described in that section.

Receiving a Charge

A volley may be fired at charging infantry or cavalry who make contact provided the charged unit is prepared to receive the charge and is in volley (Line) formation facing the chargers.

The state of readiness of the charged troops is determined by casting one die:

Cast	Result	
1	None	Troops were not prepared or
2-3-4	Half	Were demoralised by ferocity of attack
5-6	Full	Attacker must check morale

To determine the effect of a half-volley make the normal computation and divide by two, disregarding fractions. As noted, if a full volley is fired the attacker must check his morale – after all, charging into a full volley took quite a bit of guts!

In photo #13, a column has made contact in an Assault melee: the regiment receiving the charge must check its preparedness before issuing volley fire, after which the melee closes.

The regiment to the right of the charging unit will be involved by proximity, however it may fire a volley at the aggressors and, in this instance, fire an Enfilade volley!

Photo 15 French Sapeurs laying a Pontoon Bridge

Melee

The word 'melee' describes the hand-to-hand fighting of forces. It continues until one side is eliminated, surrenders or withdraws from the action.

A melee occurs when opposing troops make contact with each other. Those men within the unit(s) making contact with enemy unit(s) are the actual combatants. Other nearby troops may be involved in the melee if they are within one move of the actual combatants. Naturally, that 'move' would be for the formation they hold at the moment of melee contact. For instance, a Grenadier unit in column would be involved if it were within 6" of the actual combatants, while if that same unit were in line it would be involved only if it were within 3" of the action. Always the normal move is utilised, never a charge move for considering involvement. The same Grenadiers in column on a road leading into the action would be involved if the melee were within 9" of them. Since it is unreasonable to assume that only four or five men of a twenty man regiment would be in the action, the same 'grace area' prevails here as in volley targets: if any of the unit is within melee proximity the entire unit is involved.

To clarify, the nearby units are not physically moved to the melee area .... Only their potentially for reaching the action in one normal move is measured.

The 'moot' melee occurs when enemy units make contact through mutual charges or 'stumbling' together when neither player indicates any intent to make contact.

After determining all troops involved in the melee, it is necessary to evaluate the action. Melees are of two types: 'moot' and assault. The reason for determining the melee situation is simple: an attacker develops a shock value hereafter called 'increment' and this weight is computed in the melee.

Now for the mechanics: As previously indicated, this is a two way action with both parties fighting and assessing damage on each other which is accomplished by simultaneous dice throws and comparisons. Each player is provided with a Red die, a Green die and may elect to use a White die in lieu of the Red die if he wishes to take prisoners, which is explained under the section Prisoners. As in firing, the Red represents kills and the Green wounds. In melee, the Red (kills) is determined first, the wounds act on the survivors. In a 'moot' situation where there is no attack increment to either side, the dice are compared at face value with evaluation added if appropriate. Each die is considered separately and the difference between the pips on player A's score and B's score is affected.

Moot Melee:

Example 1: player A's throw is Red 4, Green 2 which is compared to B's Red 2, Green 1. The difference between each set of dice is the result. In this case, A has killed 2 and wounded 1 of B's men.

Example 2: In this instance player A's throw is Red 5, Green 1 which is compared to B's Red 3, Green 2. In this action A has killed 2 of B's men and B has wounded 1 of A's men.

In melees, there are two important terms: increment and evaluation. These terms do not apply to musketry since even Guardsmen's powder got wet!

Increment: The shock value built up by charging infantry (one point) or cavalry (varies with type)

Evaluation: The defensive value of a man in a melee situation, i.e., how many points the enemy must score over the unit's to injure a man. As the table following illustrates, all Infantry, with the exception of Guards, have an evaluation of one; the Guards have an evaluation of two. This means that your opponent's throw must be two points higher than yours in order to eliminate a Guardsman while other infantry require only one point to become a casualty. Cavalry vary in both their increment and evaluation.

Charge Increment & Defensive Evaluation

Personnel	Increment	Evaluation
Horse Guards/ Cuirassiers	3	3
Heavy Dragoons	2	2
Lancers*	2	1
Foot Guards	1	2
Light Horse Hussars	2	2
Light & Line Infantry	1	1
Engineers, Artillery/ Supply Troops#	1	1

*Lancers receive an extra Green die upon their initial onslaught in melee (when they institute the action) and are the only class of Cavalry which is permitted to charge an unbroken Infantry square.

These troops will participate in a charge only if attached to an Infantry unit. Basically the Special Services are not trained for melee.

Assault Melee

In this situation A's infantry has charged B's infantry which has not been ordered to charge. It does not matter what B's men have done, whether he has fallen back, changed formation, advanced a normal move or remained stationary - the attack increment goes to the man who is charging! Should A's charge carry him into contact with B's unit the battle is on. If an ordered charge does not make contact the troops are pulled back to the maximum extent of a normal move in their formation. The dice are thrown and compared once again but A may add the increment to each die, each throw of the melee. Therefore if we use our previous example #1 of A's throw: Red 4, Green 2. We actually may tabulate A's throw as Red 4 +1 = 5, Green 2+1 =3. This is then compared with B's un-incremented throw of Red 2, Green 1. The compared result: A has killed 3 and wounded 2 of B's men.

If we consider Example #2: A's throw Red 5, Green 1 becomes Red 6, Red 2 compared with B's Red 3, Green 2. The compared result is A has killed 3 of B's men while none were wounded on either side.

Evaluation Example: If, in Assault Example, #1 A is charging B's Guard unit, the die-throw becomes: A Red 4 + 1 = 5, Green 2+1 = 3 against B's Red 2 + 2 = 4, Green 1 +2 = 3. The compared result: A has killed none (two points above the Guard throw required to injure) and wounded none – the fighting was equal, negating the 'wounds' casts.

The melee action (casts of dice) continues until one side's forces are annihilated, choose to surrender, are taken prisoner, voluntarily withdraw or are forced to withdraw through morale checks.

In melee action, one may injure only the number of enemy equal to the number one has actively engaged plus their increment, i.e., if one has five men left in combat and the compared throws (including increment) would allow him to kill and wound more than five men this is not allowed unless his combatants are charging Cavalrymen having an increment of two or more.

Photo 14: Prussian and Austrian Cuirassiers charging French Line Infantry

In photo #14, the Prussian and Austrian Cuirassiers are charging French Line Infantry. Each of the three regiments of infantry facing the action must check preparedness and may then fire appropriate volleys. The column hurrying to the scene will be involved by proximity but will not participate in the firing since it is not in volley formation.

In this illustration, it is possible that the Austrian Cuirassiers making up the two rear ranks will be out of volley range yet still be part of the charge! If this is true, only the Prussians will be forced to check their morale following a full volley.

Voluntary Withdrawal

The side wishing to disengage may indicate this desire after at least one action (die throw) exchange has occurred. He announces this fact and his adversary takes one unopposed throw (including increments, if any) at the withdrawing troops after which they may retire one move toward their rear retaining the formation in which they are presently formed. The melee is then (assuming no other units are involved) considered complete. It is permissible to withdraw only one unit from action if this is desired. However, should the troops which caused withdrawal attack again on the next turn, the retiring troops must continue to withdraw, without retaliation, accepting one unopposed cast each turn. Only by the intervention of a turn free of attack by their tormentors or the introduction of fresh troops to support them may they be saved. They may engage in combat if a turn is interposed without being attacked again – however they must continue to withdraw from consecutive attacks. Units forced off the board are out of action and considered totally eliminated for 'point' purposes.

Prisoners

In an encounter of civilised peoples, there are normally prisoners resulting from the fray; there are also cases of voluntary surrender. The game affords means of depicting these occasions.

Capture

Capture may occur in only one situation that being hand-to-hand encounter.

Either party may substitute white dice for one or both dice. If a single die is substituted, it replaces the green (wounds) die and its effect is calculated in the manner of the green die, i.e., the total (including increment and/or evaluation) compared with the opponent's green die, the difference resulting in captures rather than wounds.

If desired, all dice (including extra for Enfilade) may be substituted if the player desires, or a declaration may be made that capture is desired instead of casualties, and the calculation considers the lowest number 'green' and its effect is calculated accordingly, the remaining are considered 'red' and their pips are reckoned against the opponent's throw using normal procedure.

Surrender

Voluntary surrender offers an opportunity for saving a conceivable rout of one's forces. Many a small unit would be completely wiped out to no avail if it were to engage a considerably larger force, particularly if the smaller force is isolated without support from the main body.

Notice of the desire to surrender is given before the first melee cast or the opponent casts for musketry. The situation then becomes a matter of throwing one white * die for each man wishing to surrender (*All colours may be used but their effect is considered as if all were white dice). Those scoring 5 or less are allowed to surrender; those scoring 6 are permitted to move 12" in the direction of their Headquarters unit. It is considered these men were able to move from the threatened position before consummation of the surrender.

Surrender has alleviated the possibility of the smaller unit being annihilated without opportunity to retaliate or do appreciable damage. Some of the troops have evaded this outcome to fight again. Some of the prisoners may be regained as a result of prisoner exchanges, some may be freed as they are being escorted to the prisoner 'compound'.

It may well be that surrender was the wiser course rather than a hopeless fight against overwhelming odds.

Prisoner Movement:

Prisoners are the responsibility of the captor and must be shown on the map markings. Prisoners move in column at 6" per turn under guard (one squad of line for each company of prisoners or less). Prisoners are taken to a 'compound area' near one's Headquarters and kept until an exchange agreement is reached. In games with 'point value' scoring, prisoners become of value in determining the winner's margin of victory.

Prisoner Rescues

Prisoners are 'rescued' by removing all enemy troops within musket range. Once freed, they are again the responsibility of their Commander.

Prisoners freed either by 'rescue' or exchange may not participate as combatants until they (1) have returned to their Headquarters for re-arming or, (2) are met by a supply wagon which has passed through the Headquarters area picking up arms for distribution to the returned (one regiment may be re-armed by one wagon) or, (3) claim the arms of their fallen guards.

Rescued prisoners may be recaptured. Since prisoners have no combatant value until re-armed, they would not be greatly interested in an affair which will be completely one-sided. One recaptures by the original method but since the prisoners have no way of retaliating, the capturing die-throw is unopposed. The only members of a rescued contingent who may offer any resistance are those who have been rearmed by seizing the arms of their former guards. Once the rescuers and rearmed escapees have been disposed of there is no problem in subduing the remainder.

Exchanges

Exchanges usually operate with an arrangement suitable to both parties and the prisoners involved are returned to their respective Headquarters area, or are met by supply wagons, to be re-armed. Exchanged prisoners travel through enemy territory under 'safe conduct' until 12" behind their own lines.

The relative value of units and men captured may depend largely on the number of losses from the 'stronger' side. Often a side which has suffered large numerical losses will strive to capture a key unit or person (Staff Officer or Surgeon) to have a stronger bargaining hand in the exchange.

Photo 16: Voltigeurs crossing a Pontoon Bridge

Dead and Wounded

'Dead' men and horses are removed from the field as the action which causes their demise is decided.

'Wounded' men are non-combatants. They are reclined on their side (or on a move-tray so designated) and may not participate in the fighting until they have reached the Surgeon and remained at his side or within 3" of him for one turn. Infantrymen move at the rate of 3" per move, Cavalrymen and horses move 6" per turn. Wounded are not subject to Field Regulations.

'Healed' infantrymen assemble and march back toward their front line in proper formation, resuming their normal speed, as do cavalrymen.

Wounded horses must be led to and from the hospital area. A cavalryman may lead four horses while riding one.

Special Services

Engineers

Engineers operate free of the Field Regulations and move 6" overland, 9" on roads. In addition to the normal functions of line infantry they have special abilities and functions.

Engineers may 'build' works by remaining motionless. 'Works' may be placed anywhere within 4" of the motionless engineer, one 1" section per motionless turn. Such works must be shown on the plotting surface of the player's map.

Engineers may also construct pontoon bridges, fill in fords, repair damaged works and bridges, destroy (by use of 'charges') manmade items such as works, bridges, houses.

To launch a pontoon bridge, four Engineers are required to place a one inch section per turn, thus, eight men may place two inches, twelve men may place three inches, etc.

To repair bridges damaged by artillery, two engineers per turn may repair two inches of wooden bridge surface sufficient to permit the passage of infantry or light horse, to permit the passage of artillery and heavy cavalry, four engineers per turn per two inches of repair are required. Stone bridges require three engineers per inch/turn for light repairs, five per inch/turn to make heavier repairs.

Damaged works are repaired by the original building method, one men per inch per turn, within four inches of the stationary man.

To fill in a ford crossing, two engineers and a supply wagon are required, the wagon to "transport" gravel, etc. for making the foundation. Two engineers may "fill in" one inch of stream bed wide enough to permit the passage of double-ranked infantry or an artillery team, on one turn. This is accomplished by the men in question remaining motionless one turn for each inch of ford to be built. A supply wagon may transport enough "fill" to fill three inches of stream per load.

Engineers may destroy fortifications, buildings, bridges, etc. within a diameter of a four inch circle by the placement of a "charge". It is necessary to announce when a charge is placed. The charge is placed by the engineer refraining from moving during the turn in consideration, the player then places the charge representation in the designated area; during the next turn the engineer moves his maximum distance and the charge 'explodes' killing or wounding all men within the blast circle of

4" diameter according to the Howitzer scale and destroying or damaging all constructions in the circle according, again, to the Howitzer scale. Should the engineer be killed or wounded during his stationary turn it may be assumed that the charge has been rendered inoperative and captured by an enemy touching it.

Each army has three 'charges' per Engineer to begin the game, an engineer may carry one charge with him, the rest are transported by supply wagons. Engineers 'carry' the charge by having it placed beside the figure in question and moving it along with him. Needless to say an engineer carrying a 'charge' who is hit by Howitzer or Rocket projectile immediately 'explodes' the surrounding four-inch diameter area!

Supply Wagons

Each army receives Supply wagons and personnel which may be utilised to transport supplies, ammunition personnel, casualties (wounded) or Engineers supplies (pontoon bridges, etc.). Since they move faster than Infantry, they need to offer value as troop carriers and are invaluable in shuttling ammunition and supplies between the various positions as the fortunes of war change. Where supplying the troops is a factor, it is best to arrive at the amount of supplies while each wagon may transport. In one large campaign in which the writer participated, we arrived at 25 units of supply to be transported per wagon, each unit to feed one Company of Infantry, squad of Cavalry or Artillery Battery. When wagons carry ammunition to Artillery, it is assumed each wagon can accommodate 10 rounds. At times, there may be reason to evaluate the ammunition from captured enemy artillery or damaged artillery and distribute it among the existing batteries. Remember, the ammunition delivered in these cases will be for the same calibre guns as that from which it was taken and may necessitate larger guns using the shorter trajectories or canister patterns. In no instances, will Artillery pieces use larger than rated trajectories or canister patterns.

Wagons require a minimum of one driver to move, load or unload and disburse supplies. Infantry or Cavalry replacements may be used in place of dead or wounded drivers or to drive captured wagons.

Supplies may be loaded or unloaded at the beginning of a turn, or, may move then unload. Wagons may perform two of the following three move possibilities: Load, Move, Unload. Supplies may be loaded or unloaded within a 3" circle of the wagon, disbursal is assumed to be accomplished by those receiving the supplies (who must be touching the unloaded supplies).

Cargo Destruction and Damage

Wagons utilise the sane rules of repair as Field Artillery. Cargo is not injured when the wagon is damaged, however a second consecutive 'damage' without intervening 'repair' will destroy the wagon as well as the cargo.

A wagon transporting explosives (ammunition or Sapper's charges) will be ruled destroyed along with its cargo, driver, team and passengers if an explosive shell or rocket scores a hit with 50% of the wagon body within the 'burst area' of the explosive. If a wagon is carrying explosives, a circle 6" in diameter will be adjudged as the 'blast area' and all troops (other than passengers) within the circle must be checked for injuries according to the 'Howitzer personnel damage' table.

Killing the driver or team will stop the wagon's progress until replacements are assigned and take their place.

Headquarters

Each Commander is required to set up a Command Post. He may elect to utilise a building or erect a tent. The Command post serves as the central unit and represents the Field Commander.

Headquarters (and the F.C.) move at a constant rate of 6" per turn.

Loss of the Field Commander, by any means, will bring immediate surrender of the army suffering such loss.

Staff

Staff officers (not to be confused with Line Officers who are part and parcel of the Regimental Order) are of no value except when determining morale factors. Armed with horse pistols, they may participate in Volley or Skirmisher fire if the target is within 4" of the officer. In melee, they assume the same fighting values as the men of their type (i.e. an Infantry officer is the same classification as Line, a Guard officer the same as Foot Guard, etc.).

Staff officers, being mounted, move 9" per turn.

If injured in melee, the same deduction in morale factor occurs as if the officer 'retired' from the scene: The move when wounded is 4".

Photo 17: Austrian and Prussian Field Commanders

The Field Commander does not normally participate in fighting as his loss by death or capture forces the immediate surrender of his forces. If he is wounded, deduct one point from each die in melee, Volley (add one point to green); deduct two points from Morale or skirmisher dice throws for all troops within <u>three</u> moves of the Field Commander. If the Surgeon cannot reach the side of the F.C. to 'treat' him within three moves, the army surrenders, its leadership too shaken to issue cogent orders[4].

The Field Commander has a constant move, well or wounded, of 6".

On the plus side, the presence of the Field Commander will add one point to Morale, Melee, Skirmisher casts and add one to the red die, deduct one from the green die for Volley for all troops within three moves of his position during the action.

---

[4] It was fortunate that the Prussian Army at Ligny did not feel compelled to follow this rule when Blucher was unhorsed and missing for some time!

Should the F.C. 'retire' from the scene of action through morale check, the same penalties are assessed as for his wounds.

Surgeon

The Surgeon moves at the rate of 6" per move and is a non-combatant (may not return fire if attacked). If the Surgeon is killed, the wounded may not be 'treated' and are removed from the field. If the Surgeon is wounded he may move 3" per turn and may not treat wounded for three turns. After 3 turns it is assumed his aspirin or APC has 'healed' him.

If a Surgical Staff or tent is used, the Senior Surgeon is the point of measurement and determination of 'healing' proximity.

Photo 18: Howitzer Battery of Royal Foot Artillery, Black Watch, Rifle Brigade and Life Guards

Enfilade

Credit for Enfilade may be given in melee, in volley fire and in skirmisher fire.

Enfilade defined: When an attack is launched from a point 45 degrees removed from the front of the assaulted, directly at right angles or from the rear, the assaulters may claim Enfilade. In photo 13, one instance of Enfilade volley is illustrated. Photos 16 and 17 are instances of Enfilade volley with the French line firing into the Prussians.

To calculate Enfilade volley an extra red die is awarded and the killing potential is based on the two red dice combined. The effect can be quite dramatic!

Photos 18 and 19 are instances of Enfilade melee. In these instances an extra red die is awarded the group assaulting on the first melee throw only. Lancers, when claiming Enfilade, would cast two red dice and two green dice on the initial assault.

In photo #20, skirmisher fire is being delivered at Enfilade. In this instance, two points are added to the dice throw of the individual firers.

Units exposed to Enfilade on a breakthrough (except for broken squares) are not subject to Enfilade on the breakthrough unless they are frontally engaged in melee and the unit breaking through is capable of reaching their rear in one normal move.

This has happened in the past and no doubt will occur at some time in your games: Player A has a unit of infantry in column, poised to assault B's line; B has a unit of troops perpendicular to the route over which A's troops must pass. When the maps are marked A has shown his charge into B's line, but B has shown an Enfilade charge to intercept A's charging unit. To properly decide whether or not an Enfilade may be claimed, measure from the starting positions of each unit, the unit having the farthest distance to travel to reach the intercept point is assumed to have hit the flank of their adversaries. In the example given, B has clearly shown an intention of Enfilade assault and should properly have the Enfilade credit since it is assumed his Regimental Commander would have held his charge until the enemy's flank were exposed. In cases where 'moot' melees occur, use the 'farthest distance' rule.

Frankly, I am against throwing dice to decide points which may be settled by logic.

Superior Position

When forces oppose one another on a field with no protective advantage to either party, this is an 'open position'.

When the lay of the land or man-made formation gives material advantage to one side or the other, some facility must be available to represent the superiority of that position. Therefore, when an attack is launched upon a defending party situated in a position which logically would give them some protection from the attackers, a compensation is made in the weight of the attacker's effectiveness by the removal of value in dice thrown. This advantage operates for the attackers when an attack is launched from a similar position.

The following scale represents the penalisation exacted in various Superior Positions. Remember, the Superior Position merely hampers the effectiveness of the group operating against it; it does not give an increment to the group within it although this is the effect created.

Forfeit Against Superior Position

Melee:

Position	Red Die Forfeit	Green Die Forfeit
Elevation	1	0
Woods	1	1
Masonry (Buildings)	2	1
Formations	2	1
Works	2	2

Volley:

Position	Red Die Forfeit	Add to Green Die
Elevation	1	0
Woods	1	1
Masonry (Buildings)	2	1
Formations	2	1
Works	2	2

Skirmisher:

Position	Required to Wound	Required to Kill
Elevation	7-8-9	10-11-12
Woods	8-9-10	11-12
Masonry (Buildings)	9-10	11-12
Formations	9-10	11-12
Works	9-10	11-12

When troops remove from a Superior Position penalisation is removed. Superior Position protection remains so long as any troops remain in position for which credit has been received.

If both groups involved in a situation (i.e. firing or fighting) or should an attacking group gain access to the position, they do not negate one another, but both operate under the handicap.

Withdrawal privileges are still available to those in a Superior Position. They may find their situation untenable and choose to remove rather than suffer further casualties.

It is possible there may be a combination of Superior Position factors and it is the responsibility of the Commander whose forces are in the position to claim all the protection he can before the first cast of the dice.

The British Foot Artillery shown in photo #18 has combined Superior Position advantages, being emplaced in works on an elevation. Should an attack be launched against them, two factors will work against the attackers until (1) the works are breached by Artillery or Engineer's charges and (2) the attackers succeed in climbing the elevation and passing the works unopposed by defenders.

Superior Positions may be outflanked and when this occurs, they no longer penalise the attackers – indeed, should the line of fire be open, the defenders may be subject to Enfilade!

Masonry (buildings) works, formations or woods may be destroyed and removed by Artillery or Engineer's explosives and once breached no longer serve as advantages against attacking troops in the area of their destruction unless repaired or replaced by Engineers. The Superior Position claim, when removed, exposes the defenders to fire. Explosive shells may remove personnel within the 'burst area' circle; similarly for men within the circle of an engineer's charge. Solid shot removes the cover through the proper number of damage hits but does not injure personnel on the initial firing. Canister fired into woods or heavy underbrush (which must be designated) injures the troops on the following scale:

6	Dead
4-5	Wounded
1-2-3	Unharmed

Canister fired into works, masonry (building) or formations is calculated as: 6 – wounded; lesser pips, unharmed. An attacker may choose to fire only against those newly exposed by recent Artillery fire, and against this group only; he may use the full value of the toss without forfeit for position. He may not include still-protected troops in this calculation even though they are included in the pattern. In some cases, even though the defence has been breached, the attacker may be content to fire on the whole group and operate with the disadvantage.

It is impossible to anticipate the many combinations and problems that can arise from the matter of Superior Position and its ramifications but this variance of situation is one of the strongest interest points of the game. Most of the questions arising from the matter can be answered by common sense and logic.

Superior Position Defined

Elevation: When troops rest on a higher level than the enemy, they may claim elevation until those on the elevation have been removed. Charges launched from an elevation only build up impetus as recognised in the increment given descending heights. For an attacker to claim elevation, he must make contact while having assault troops in the elevated position.

Woods: Only specifically indicated woods may qualify for the claim - a line is to be drawn around the area considered Superior Position. Single stands of trees may not qualify. Areas of heavy underbrush, where defined, will operate against musketry or canister but not against melee.

Masonry and Buildings: This applies to man-made stonelike (or frame) situations, buildings, or the ruins of them. To claim Masonry or Buildings, the men making the claim must have part of the structure interposed between them and the line of fire. It is not satisfactory to merely be within the ruin or building, one must be shielded. Buildings of solid construction are discounted as defensive Superior Positions except as shielding against fire. 'Take-apart' buildings in which troops may be placed in such a manner to return fire receive the same advantage as Masonry.

Buildings set afire by Rockets or Explosive Shells subject the men inside to injury in the following manner:

When the projectile lands on the roof of the building, shake one die and use the following:

1   All killed, none escape (Building collapsed inward)

2-3 1/3 killed, 1/3 wounded, 1/3 escape

4-5 1/3 wounded, remainder escape

6   All escape, none harmed.

If an explosive shell lands at the side of the building (with burst area covering the major part of the wall), the die cast is:

1   All men in the building wounded by falling wall

2-3   Men on the side of blast wounded by falling wall

4-5-6 No injuries

Works and Forts: These are man-made constructions for the specific purpose of defence. They may be stockades or forts or may be a combination of trenches/breastworks constructed by Engineers. To receive the claim the men must be behind the fortifications as in the Masonry concept.

Formations: Formations are natural defences of nature's doing, stones providing cover, rills, ditches, depressions, etc. One must be shielded as in the Masonry section to receive the claim.

Time Factors

In an actual encounter, decisions must often be made in minutes and let the commander hope he is right. So it should be on the wargame table! When actual contact is made, time becomes even more valuable and the commander who cannot think fast and with some degree of accuracy should be placed at a disadvantage. Assuming that every commander goes into battle after carefully studying the terrain situation and forming a 'master plan', let us set a time limit for marking the moves on the plotting surface and then, for actually getting one's forces into proper position.

An ordinary kitchen timer with a bell serves very satisfactorily for this purpose. Until actual contact is made, I propose a maximum of fifteen minutes be allowed to mark the plotting surface and, unless cards are being used - which can (or should) be moved into position in a matter of seconds - an additional fifteen minutes be allowed after the time signal sounds for men to be placed in their proper position. Of course, if you are moving vast numbers without the aid of moving stands, some extra physical moving time may be allotted.

After contact is actually made, time for marking maps should be reduced to ten minutes! The logic and reasons are obvious: one either learns to make the proper decisions quickly under pressure or becomes a consistent loser!

You may wish to experiment with these time limits and arrive at one to suit your group of players – let me assure you, nothing adds boredom and exasperation to the game so much as waiting for a player to make up his mind. Wargames have consumed up to fifteen hours that, logically, should have been completed in five hours at the outside!

Night (or Concealed Movement)

The card layout system is utilised here, carrying through much farther. The cards may be broken down to represent the smallest operational entity (Squad, Company, or Regiment) and move across the field at those units' rates. When within 18" of an enemy unit the card is then revealed. Artillery range is reduced, actually, since the same measuring trajectory sticks are used, but targets beyond this range are 'shrouded in darkness'. If a projectile is fired and bounces onto an undisplayed unit, that unit must be placed on the board and casualties assessed! Larger pieces (#8, 12#) will probably wish to use the Horse Artillery trajectory.

Random Entry-Reinforcements

You will note on the Melee Layout illustration, there are eleven numbered sections on each side of the table, numbered 2-12.

If desired, a Commander may hold part of his forces in reserve at the beginning of the game; however, he must announce, or may choose to do so with a sealed envelope marked to be opened on the --- move, when they will be introduced to the scene. On a slip of paper inside the envelope, he must have a number from 2-12 written and introduce the new units at that point.

Die Throw Entry

An announcement may be made at the start of play: 'I have --- units which will be entered at random during play'.

When the Commander desires to enter one or more units, he will announce the fact and throw two dice – the unit(s) must enter the field at that designated sector – and good luck!

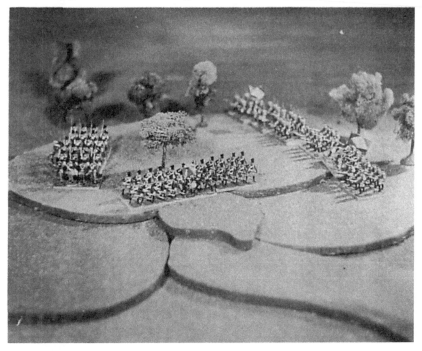

Photo: 19 French Line firing an Enfilade volley at Prussian Line

Forced Marches

The Guardsmen, both foot and horse and certain other units, were chosen for their stamina. On many occasions, Napoleon's Guard made staggering-to-contemplate forced marches covering several days.

In our game, we allow the Guards, both foot and horse, Light Infantry, Rifles and Scout Lancers, one forced march move every tenth game move with the following limitations:

Foot Units	18"
Horse Units	27" Guards
	48" Scout Lancers

At the end of the 'forced march', the units may not participate in a Charge until one turn has passed and may participate in action only if attacked! If these units pass within musketry range of an enemy force while en route, they must accept the musketry (volley will probably be at Enfilade!) without pausing to retaliate, in other words, they are needed desperately somewhere and they get there, fast!

Foot units will forced march in close order road column formation; horse in close order 'trot' formation. No dispersal will be allowed!

War at Sea

Photo 20: Frigates in close support at La Fere

Much of the research information for this section has been found in the *'Naval History of Great Britain'*, by William James, first published in 1837.

Ships are rated according to the number of broadside guns carried and by rigging. By the dawn of the nineteenth century, it was generally agreed that a ship, by definition, was a vessel having three masts and square-rigged.

Ship-of-the-line or line-of-battle ship was a rating of itself with subsidiary ratings within it. By 1800, the ratings were:

	First Rate	100 carriage guns	Three gundecks
	Second Rate	90-98 carriage guns	Three gundecks
S.O.L	Third Rate	64-84 carriage guns	Two gundecks
	Fourth Rate	50 carriage guns	Two gundecks
	Fifth Rate	32-44 carriage guns	One gundeck
Frigate	Sixth Rate	20-28 carriage guns	One gundeck
Sloop	No rating	14-18 carriage guns	One gundeck

Note: The ratings are for Carriage-guns.

The names of ships' masts are: Fore (front), Main (centre) and Mizzen (rear). On those having four masts, the stern most one was called the Bonaventure Mizzen or Bonaventure.

In 1779, General Robert Melville developed and cast a new gun at the foundry of the Carron Company in Scotland. Due to improved manufacturing methods, the gun was able to fire a larger projectile from a barrel of much less weight and length than the guns currently mounted abroad ships. Of this gun James writes: 'The new gun had now taken the name of Carronade, and its several varieties became distinguished, like those of the old gun, by the weight of their respective shot. This occasioned the smasher to be called, irrevocably, a 68 pounder: whereas repeated experiments had shown, that a hollow or cored shot, weighing

50, or even 40lbs., would range further in the first graze, or that which the shot first strikes the surface of the water, and the only range worth attending to in naval gunnery. The hollow shot would also, owing to its diminished velocity in passing through a ship's side, and the consequent enlargement of the hole and increased splintering of the timbers, produce more destructive effects than the shot in its solid form; one of the principal objections against which was, and still continues to be, its being so cumbrous to handle!'

Further, James notes: 'Still the Board of Ordnance, in repeated conferences with the Navy Board, maintained the superiority of the old gun, resting their arguments chiefly on the comparative length of its range; while the Navy Board urges a vessel, able to carry 4 pounders of the common construction might, with equal ease, bear 18 pounders of the new that the latter gun was far more formidable and destructive; and that its range was quite sufficient for the purpose required.'

Long guns and Carronades came to be placed abroad ships of the British navy. One of the first frigates to be outfitted with both was HMS Rainbow which was rated as a 44-gunner.

	Long Guns		Carronades	
First Deck	20	18 pdrs	20	68 pdrs
Second Deck	22	12 pdrs	22	42 pdrs
Quarterdeck	--	--	4	32 pdrs
Forecastle	2	6 pdrs	2	32 pdrs
Total	44	818 pds	48	1238 pds

Thus a 44 gun rated Frigate mounted a total of 92 guns with a broadside weight-of-metal of 1556 pounds.

The first combat use of carronades occurred when the Rainbow met the French frigate, Hebe, on September 4, 1783. James gives this account: 'Owing to the latter's peculiar bearing, one of the Rainbow's forecastle 32 pounders was first discharged at her. Several of the shot fell on board, and discovered their size. The French captain, rationally concluded that, if such large shot came from the forecastle of the enemy's ship, much larger ones would follow from her lower batteries, fired his broadside 'pour l'honneur de pavilion' and surrendered to the Rainbow. Although the capture of the Hebe had offered no opportunity of trying the experiment contemplated by the Navy Board, and so ardently looked forward to by the officers and crew of the Rainbow, yet did the prize, in the end, prove a most valuable acquisition to the service, there being very few British frigates, even of the present day (1837), which in size and exterior form, are not copied from the Hebe. She measured 1063 tons, and mounted 40 guns, twenty-eight 18, and twelve 8 pounders.'

Eventually Carronades were added to the ordnance of all navies. The number of 'carriage guns' determined ratings so we find instances where ships might have 150 muzzles from which to discharge missiles but bear only a '100 gun' rating. The Carronades were usually mounted on the forecastle as bow chasers and quarterdeck or poop deck as stern chasers.

Long before, 5" mortar shells had been fired from 'long guns', now the stubby-barrelled Carronades were found better suited for this purpose.

The French navy had the following ratings in guns, Carronades and crews:

Ships-of-the-Line

Gun Rate		120	110	80	74
Main Deck	No.	32	30	30	28
	Pds	36	36	36	36
2nd Deck	No.	34	32	32	30
	Pds	24	24	24	24
3rd Deck	No.	34	32	--	--
	Pds	12	12	--	--
Quarter	No.	14	12	12	12
	Pds	8	8	12	8
Fo'c'sle	No.	6	4	6	4
	Pds	8	8	12	8
Poop Carronades	No.	4	4	6	4
	Pds	36	36	36	36
Crews numbered (officers and men)		1098	1037	840	690

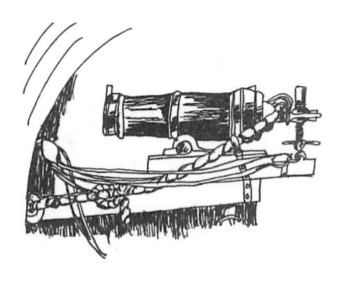

Frigates

Gun Rate		40	38	36	32	28
Main Deck	No.	28	26	26	26	24
	Pds	18	18	12	12	8
Quarterdeck guns	No.	10	10	8	4	-
	Pds	8	8	6	6	-
Quarterdeck Carronades	No.	2	2	2	2	6
	Pds	8	36	36	36	36
Forecastle	No.	2	2	2	2	2
	Pds	36	8	6	6	6
Carronades	No.	2	2	2	36	-
	Pds	36	36	36	2	-
Crews numbered (officers and men)		320	320	300	275	200

Of the small amount of stern ordnance, James says: 'There is one remarkable peculiarity in the arrangement of the guns on board of French ships. So paramount to all other considerations is the comfort of the captain, that no guns are mounted in the cabin of a line-of-battle ship; and sometimes the aftermost port of the main deck is left vacant to answer a similar purpose.'

French ships mounting fewer than 28 'long guns' were classified as Corvettes, Brig-Corvettes, Brigantines or Avisos.

All navies had auxiliary ships: hospital, supply and gun-boats.

Shipboard ammunition consisted of solid roundshot, grape, bar shot, chain-shot and 'bombs' or explosive shells.

In one instance of a frigate versus frigate encounter, the ammunition expelled by the British frigate was 36 half-barrels of powder, 842 solid shot, 72 grape-shot in cases, 70 case shot, 50 double-headed (bar) shot, 500 musket balls and 150 pistol balls. This action, between the British 'Boston' and French 'Embuscade' was inconclusive!

'Carriage Guns' referred to regular Navy ordnance mounted on trucks and excluded truck-mounted Carronades. The same mounting system was in use abroad ships and at most fortresses of the time. Most

Carronades were mounted on a platform with the gun on a sliding base as per the sketch above (not the one later below). In general, Carronades were served by smaller gun crews.

I have found little information referring to the range of Carronades. Janes defines gun-shot range as: '... a ship is within gunshot of another when she is within a mile or a mile-and-a-quarter of her.' He makes no reference to the calibre of the gun.

Ships in the Game

In our game, we have three classes of fighting ships: Ship-of-the-line, Frigate and Brig.

Ship-of-the-Line:

For use in games where men on shore are involved, the ship-of-the line is three-masted, 24" long and 10" wide. She carries four longboats for purposes of towing when becalmed. Ten men are required to man each long-boat for towing purposes.

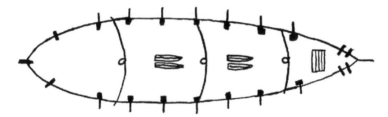

Her full game crew consists of 20 companies of sailors and 10 companies of marines. Sailors and marines man the broadside guns and rockets.

The four longboats are carried between the fore and main and main and mizzen masts.

Four 68-pound Carronades are mounted on her forecastle and three on the quarterdeck. Seven 42-pound long guns are on each broadside. A five tube rocket launcher is forward of the foremast.

Frigate

Frigates are also three-masted but are 18" long and 8" wide. A Frigate carries two long boats; again, ten men are required per boat for towing a becalmed ship.

Her full crew is made up of 10 companies of sailors and 5 companies of marines.

Long boats are carried between the masts.

A Frigate mounts three 42 pound Carronades forward and two aft. Four 12 pound long guns are mounted on each broadside. A five-tube rocket launcher is forward of the foremast.

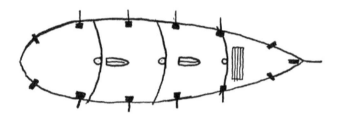

Brig

The Brig is two-masted, 12" long and 6" wide, and carries one longboat.

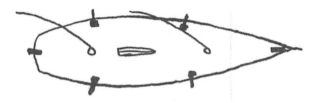

Brigs are manned by 5 companies of sailors, have a 32 pound Carronade forward and another aft, and two 8 pound long guns on each broadside.

Longboats

Longboats may tow ships 3" per boat per turn for S. O. L., 4" per boat per turn for Frigates and 5" per boat per turn for Brigs. Ships may continue firing while being towed. Towing longboats are placed 6" ahead of the ship.

When towing, longboats present a target 3" long and 1-1½" wide. One hit by any ordnance except rocket sinks a longboat with all hands.

Longboats may transport one Carronade (any calibre) or a 12 pound gun plus 10 marines ashore. Longboats thus loaded move 6" per turn, empty, 10".

When Carronades are landed ashore, they may be moved by hand 1" per turn if a minimum of 6 men are available. They may not fire while in longboats.

Truck mounted Carronade

Ship-to-shore Firing and Fighting

Ship Move Distances

Brigs move 36" per turn

Frigates move 24" per turn

Ships-of-the-line move 18" per turn

Ships may change course 90 degrees during a turn but forfeit half their move distance.

In the following section are methods of determining changes in wind and sea conditions. If one does not wish to employ these changes, the above distances remain constant.

Unless anchored, ships must move each turn. One move is required to anchor. To weigh anchor, a full turn is required and the following losses in move distance on the move following:

Brig 12", Frigate 8", S. O. L. 6"

When firing against shore batteries, the same rules of damage are used as for field artillery. Guns are fired and damage assessed individually. Carronades may swivel 180 degrees to fire, but not toward masts. Long guns are restricted to firing 10 degrees to either side, perpendicular to the axis of the ship.

Rockets may be fired to either side or ahead but not astern.

32-pound Carronades use the same trajectory stick as the 12 pound gun for solid rounds. The 'splash' point is 22½" from the muzzle. When the 32-pound Carronade fires explosive shells their maximum range is 25" and damage is assessed according to the Howitzer scale and blast circle. The 32-pounder also uses the Howitzer canister pattern.

42-pound Carronades use the 24-pound field gun trajectory stick. The 'splash' point is 30" from the muzzle. When firing explosive shells the maximum range is 30". Damage from explosive shells and firing grape follows the same rules as for the Howitzer.

The 42-pound long gun and 68-pound Carronade use the trajectory stick below:

35"	5"	4"	12"	5"	6"	1½"
White	Red	W	Red	W	Green	

The 'splash' point is 37" from the muzzle for both.

Maximum range for firing explosives from the 68-pound Carronade is 40". Damage from explosive shells and firing grape follows the same rules as for the Howitzer.

Fortress Guns:

Fortresses will be allotted the following ordnance:

Four 42-pound guns

Six 24-pound guns

Six 6" Howitzers

It is assumed guns are truck-mounted (which was normal) but they may swivel 45 degrees. If it is desired to shift a fortress gun from one position on the wall to another, ten men are required to move the gun one inch per turn. (Remember, a 12 pounder truck gun weighed around 3,500 pounds!)

To achieve uniformity, let us assume fortress walls are equivalent to 4 contours of height. The rough dimensions below fit our scale:

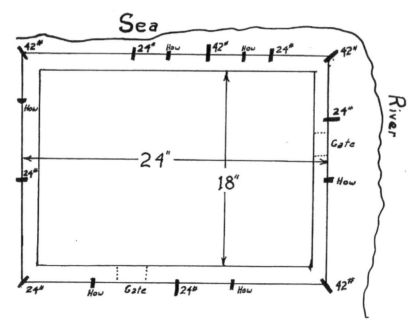

Gun replacement is suggested. Most ordnance guards the sea and river approaches; the landward approach is assumedly guarded by land forces.

Guns may be shifted along the walls. The top of the wall is wide enough to permit dragging one gun behind another, but not while firing the gun the moving gun is behind.

Shore Gun Damage to Ships

As noted, ships damage ordnance ashore according to the Field Artillery damage scale.

When shore guns fire at a ship, the normal windage gauge is used, with a point on the ship selected as the target.

When firing shore guns at a ship, after determining windage, throw one die, the projectile strikes the ship (assuming it is in range):

5-6 Waterline Hit

3-4 Freeboard Hit

1-2 Rigging Hit

A ship can absorb two rigging hits per mast before its move distance is shortened. After absorbing these hits, deduct 4" from the move distance for each additional rigging hit until the ship is becalmed.

Freeboard hits will not slow a ship's progress but will destroy a ship's guns if the gun is within 1" of the hit area. Using the field artillery scale, a 5 or 6 scored on one die will destroy the gun in question; 3 or 4 will damage it. Guns are repaired according to field artillery rules, remaining inactive for two full turns.

If use of the windage calculator and placement die puts a solid shot into a ship's mast, a single die score of 5 or 6 removes the mast; 3 or 4 damages the mast. Three damages remove a mast. Masts cannot be repaired under fire. For each mast lost, deduct the appropriate distance from the move.

Ships may absorb the following waterline hits on one side before sinking:

S. O. L.   6

Frigate   4

Brig   2

Ships' rockets have the same range and effectiveness as field rockets. A rocket hitting a ship's rigging counts as three rigging hits, it being assumed the rocket will set the rigging afire. Rockets hitting the waterline do NO damage! Rockets hitting on deck will start a fire with a single die throw of 6; if another rocket or howitzer hits the same area within three turns, the ship is in danger and must withdraw.

Howitzer shells hitting in the rigging count as quadruple hits. Howitzer shells landing on deck will dismast a ship if the mast is in the blast circle. Ships' guns within the howitzer blast circle are destroyed. Three howitzer shells within the same area within three turns force a ship to withdraw afire.

Three waterline hits by howitzers will sink a ship-of-the-line, two a frigate, one a brig. A howitzer waterline hit must be called for when estimating range, if the range is less than one inch short, the waterline hit is allowed, if more than 1" over, the shell exploded on deck.

Assessing personnel casualties in ship-to-shore duels is relatively unimportant since the object is to sink the ship or silence shore batteries.

Assaulting a beach under fire was seldom attempted in this time period. If a battle ensued, the ships carrying troops, unless of fighting class, lay off at a safe distance from the shore, whether engaging in a duel with shore guns or protecting the fleet.

Ship-to-ship Firing and Fighting

A smaller scale is used here, and it is assumed no fortress guns or shore guns are in use.

Small cardboard models of ships may be made to the following dimensions:

S. O. L. 6" long, 3" wide; Frigate 4" long, 2" wide; Brig 3" long, 1" wide.

The ship-of-the-line mounts 48 guns, 24 to a side, with a firing range of 12", and has a basic move 9" per turn.

Frigates mount 24 guns, 12 to a side, with a firing range of 9", and have a basic move of 12".

Brigs mount 12 guns, 6 to a side, with a firing range of 6", and have a basic move 15".

Ships fire broadsides only; they may fire one broadside from each side per turn.

Wind and Sea Conditions

Wind direction and velocity is determined every fifth move in the following manner:

Direction: throw one die

2 North 3 East 4 South 5 West (1 or 6 throw again)

Velocity: throw one die

1 Dead calm, longboats tow a Brig 3", a Frigate 2", or a S. O. L. 1"

2-3-4 Ideal sailing conditions

5 Stormy

6 Full Gale

Ship Move Distances

The basic move is allowed ships under ideal sailing conditions when sailing across the wind; move distances vary when sailing with the wind, tacking into the wind, or under other than ideal conditions according to the following chart:

Ship's Direction

Wind Velocity	With Wind	Across Wind	Into Wind
2	0	0	0
3	Add 1"	0	Deduct 1"
4	Add 2"	0	Deduct 2"
5	Add 5"	Add 3"	Deduct 4"
6	Add 8"	Add 5"	Deduct 6"

If ships pass within broadside range of each other during a move, broadsides are automatically exchanged unless one of the ships has indicated holding its broadside for a particular target.

Broadside effectiveness is determined by throwing two dice: for a Brig divide the score by two to determine the number of hits on the target; the total score determines the hits for a Frigate; for ships-of-the line, multiply the score by two.

If more than half the shots fired hit the target, throw one die to determine the area of the ship damaged:

5-6 Waterline Hit

3-4 Freeboard Hit

1-2 Rigging Hit

Each rigging hit per mast will slow the ship one inch per turn, eventually forcing movement by longboat.

With each freeboard hit, deduct one pip from subsequent broadsides fired from that side of the ship.

Four waterline hits sink a Brig, six a Frigate and eight a S. O. L. However, a full broadside fired from a ship of equal or larger class hitting the waterline sinks the ship.

Each damage should be marked on the ships.

Boarding and Capturing

In the reduced scale, ship's complements are:

Brig: Three companies sailors

Frigate: Five companies sailors, 5 companies marines

If ships collide accidentally, a 'moot melee' situation follows involving the entire crews of both ships. One or both ships may withdraw one-half its allowed move distance if the player states such a desire and accepts one opposed throw.

Records of casualties in such melees should be kept until the full action is completed.

If a player marks his map with the intent of boarding and capturing an enemy vessel, the following mechanics are used:

If contact is made, a 'boarding party' is sent over, Brigs will dispatch two companies of sailors; Frigates, three companies of sailors and two companies of marines; and S. O. L., five companies of sailors and four companies of marines.

The player indicating 'boarding' receives an increment of one for sailors, and two for marines in action. Action is the same as an 'assault melee' with the exception of doubles. Should doubles be thrown, the person against whom they are thrown will deduct one pip from each die on the next throw.

If the boarding is successful, the survivors of the boarding party (which may not be over one-half of the entire crew) may operate their prize, firing one broadside (all guns on one side) per turn thereafter; the same for the 'stripped' crew of the capturing ship. Should they choose, captor and prize may attempt to leave the area, and should they succeed in sailing 'off the board', their escape is made good.

If the boarding party wishes to withdraw, he indicates the intention and accepts one unopposed toss of the dice. The boarded ship may then attempt a boarding and will succeed if two dice throws total 9 or more.

Ships must disengage from action, by attempting to leave the area, if their crews suffer casualties which leave fewer than:

Brigs: One company total

Frigates: Two companies total

S. O. L.   Three companies total

Squadron and Fleet sizes

In Napoleonic times, a 'fleet' was considered any number of ships over ten, a 'squadron' or 'division' any lesser number having at least one S. O. L. or Frigate with a post-captain commanding. In our game, a 'squadron' is

4 S. O. L.

2 Frigates

2 Brigs

Two squadrons constitute a flotilla; two flotillas a fleet.

The ship-of-the-line was the important factor. Frigates were used for scouting purposes. Nelson said, 'Send me more eyes!' when requesting additional frigates for his fleet cruising the Mediterranean in search of the French. Brigs or sloops were used as messenger ships.

Summation

I realise that, when compared to the rest of the book, the naval rules are somewhat crude. Most of them have been worked out in solo games since few persons are interested in playing naval wargames set in the Napoleonic period[5].

Twenty-four pound Truck Gun

---

[5]The variety of model ships and wargame rules available today suggests this is no longer the case! When this book was written, however, the lack of suitable models and rules may simply have prevented many wargamers from pursuing their interest in naval warfare.

International Wars

This section is written to give a point from which to work when a game involving several players is desired.

'International Wars' can be played between persons in the same general area or scattered across the globe. One game-by-mail of my knowledge involved players in California, Illinois, Pennsylvania, England and Arabia!

The minimum number of participants is four. It is recommended there be no more than twelve players in the game.

Each player is a 'National Leader' and should have the privilege of defending his own soil. A player may ask another to be his 'Field Commander' when attacking another 'nation'. In games-by-mail it is customary for persons in one area to choose their F.C. ahead of the invasion in order to give him all information required to carry put the planned operation.

Umpire

For obvious reasons, it is best if the Umpire does not participate as a player in the game.

To the Umpire goes the job of settling questions which invariably arise in the game. For this reason, he should always be kept informed of the strength and movements of each player's forces. He should have a full report of each battle, and both sides' losses or gains.

The Umpire may operate an 'espionage service'. Players inquiring about other players' forces or intentions would receive multiple answers, one of which would be correct. On occasion, to add a dash of spice and keep things stirred up, the Umpire may choose to operate an 'agitation' service!

When the game is being set up, the Umpire should have the opportunity to suggest rules which could make his job easier. Once the game is underway, changes may be called for and the Umpire should announce the change with the whys and wherefores.

Maps

Each participant should have a scale map of the 'world' in which the game takes place. The map should be as detailed as possible, showing all cities, roads, islands, mountains and forests.

Beginning the Game

Each 'nation' begins the game with equal strength and potential. This is a bit unrealistic when compared to our international situation but makes a much better game. The better players, or those who choose the better F.C.'s to handle their invasions, will eventually come out on top, just as in actuality.

At the start of the game, a Defence Division should be stationed at each 'homeland' city and 'original' colony. Defence Divisions never operate out of the 'city boundary', which is usually a day's march. Their purpose is to defend the city when attacked.

Each nation begins the game with an equal number of Attack Divisions, usually four. Attack Divisions are used as aggressive forces, to establish new colonies, to attempt the recapture of fallen homeland cities or colonies. When Attack Divisions march out of their country, they have supplies for two weeks only. Within this time period, they must meet another division which may share supplies, capture an enemy city or colony, establish a new colony, or return to a homeland city or colony, or be forced to surrender to the closet 'foreign' power for lack of supplies. While Attack Divisions are in the field, a line of communication and supply must be kept open to their nearest homeland city or a head which may be supplied by their ships. If an enemy unit succeeds in cutting off the line of supply or communication, the unit has one week to clear the line, regardless of possession of an enemy city.

Defence and Attack Fleets are also required. Their seagoing purposes parallel the land divisions. However, fleets may cruise and operate together as a combined force.

Transports are required for troops dispatched by sea. It is easiest to assume transports are always available for each Attack Division; four are required to transport a Division with two weeks' supplies. In the case of an unescorted transport fleet meeting an enemy fleet, since the transports are unarmed they must either make a safe harbour without the enemy fleet coming within five miles of them or half the division is deemed lost at sea, the remainder is captured with half its artillery.

Division and Fleet Types

For more interesting Divisional battle and Fleet Battles it is suggested that a variety of Divisional and Fleet types be agreed upon. Each N.L. should decide upon the composition of his original Divisions and Fleets and, of course, the composition of resupply or bonus Fleets and

Divisions. Once their composition has been chosen for Fleets or Divisions, their organisation remains the same, even when rebuilding following a battle.

Time Element

Each normal calendar day may represent either one or two game days. Depending on the distance separating the players to allow exchange of mail, a day-is-a-day is usual. If all players live within a small radius where telephone communication is not too expensive, one day could easily represent two game days[6].

When an invasion is launched and troops are in battle proximity, a 'time freeze' should go into effect in that area until the battle is fought. Except in cases of emergency trips or vacations, two weeks will allow plenty of time for the defender to prepare maps and meet in battle. If there are no extenuating circumstances, a delay of longer than two weeks should result in a forfeit of the battle by the defender with an automatic loss of one-half Division.

Gaining new Troops and Fleets

Those experienced in 'International' games have found it best to rule that no country may gain new forces unless it has participated in a battle during the preceding month. This discouraged those who are inclined to sit and grow fat until their neighbours are worn down with fighting, then pour in a flood on them in the form of 'unearned' Divisions!

For easier bookkeeping, it has been found best to organise Divisions so that losses may be determined in quarter-units. Bonus points for winning battles, points for cities, both homeland and captive, and points for colonies may then be awarded in quarter-units keeping records as simple as possible.

Resupply should be allowed once each game month. The amount of new supplies should be based on the value of 'real estate' in possession on the first of the new month. If resupply points are given in quarter-units, the following is suggested:

- For each conquered enemy homeland city:

---

[6] Email would probably be players' preferred method of communication these days, but the fundamental principles of a play by mail campaign remain the same.

1 Division OR quarter S.O.L. OR half Frigate OR 1Brig

- For each captured enemy colony:

three quarters Division OR quarter S.O.L. OR half Frigate OR 1 Brig.

- For each 'Homeland' city intact:

half Division OR quarter Frigate OR half Brig

- For each original or newly established colony*

quarter Division OR quarter Frigate OR half Brig

Bonus Points

For each land engagement won:

Half a Division, plus half the enemy's operable artillery at the end of the battle. Each Division may capture and use artillery, building its artillery to not more than 150% of its original. Any artillery above this amount may be transported to another Division or city.

For each Naval engagement won:

All captured enemy ships plus half S.O.L., one Frigate, one and a half Brigs

Naval bonus points should only bring the country back to its original strength. Captured enemy ships, if lost in battle, are not resupplied.

*New colonies should not be established closer than one day's sailing or five days' marching time to the homeland, captive city, captive colony, or original colony. To gain resupply points a new colony should be established at the beginning of the game.

Alliances and Power Bloc

Although they certainly exist in reality, alliances and power blocs only bring alienation and confusion to wargames. The hiring of 'mercenaries' may be allowed in the form of Divisions, ships or captured artillery, but a limit should be established at the beginning of the game.

Non-aggression pacts are allowable and, as in real life, may be broken at any time!

Battles for Cities

It is recommended that all battles take place outside the city proper, that sieges not be allowed.

The defending army may have one third of its forces two move distances on the table (sentries at advanced positions) at the beginning of play and the attacker not more than a quarter as an advance guard and scouts. Since the advanced posts would be somewhat prepared it is permissible for the homeland forces to have a minimum of prepared defensive positions on the field of play.

Let us assume the map below is that of a nation in an 'International' wargame. Largmouthana has invaded Tryptagolia, crossing the border and passing through the town of Pfut. The capital city, Trypton, is now five days' march away! The invasion is accompanied by a formal declaration of war.

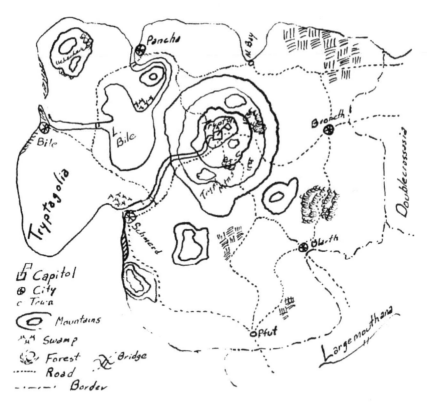

Each map contour equals two table contours

The procedure, thus far would be for Largemouthana to previously notify the umpire of its decision to declare war on Tryptagolia, sending a copy of its troops' 'marching orders' which clearly outline their route. Largemouthana may have one, two, three or four divisions *en route* but their spacing and route must be clearly given to the umpire.

Tryptagolia will be notified that it has been invaded and at what point, but the numbers and types of divisions will not be revealed until Tryptagolia meets each of them in combat. Pfut, being a town, would not have a Defensive Division, therefore the invaders march through unopposed.

If Tryptagolia has an Attack Division which is able to intercept the invaders, an open field battle takes place with no prepared works allowed, and each army could begin the game with a quarter of its forces – advance guards - two move distances on the table.

Assuming there is no interception, the invaders march toward the capital. Let us assume that one day's march from the capital in the direction of the threat places the centre of the field of battle at the point where the road crosses the third contour level of the Trypt Mts., just beside the 's'. The layout map for the battle might show:

This is an interesting terrain to attack but not impossible. The defender has prepared redoubts flanking the highway and no doubt his engineers will join them by spanning the Royale Pike with works.

The attacker has a slope to overcome and woods constituting a Superior Position against which he may have to operate, or may be able to use for his advantage, yet there is enough room for him to outflank the defences.

Assuming the Largemouthana Commander desires to gamble, he may be permitted to detach his faster units at the point where the road curves behind the first wooded area on the large map and send them directly cross-country toward the supposed point of intercept. He must write his orders, stating clearly where the unit(s) will leave and rejoin the main body. He then must calculate the daily movement of both contingents and, if his guess is right, may bring the detached units on the table at point A sometime during the battle. Couriers mounted on fast horses are available to pursue the detached elements and change their orders.

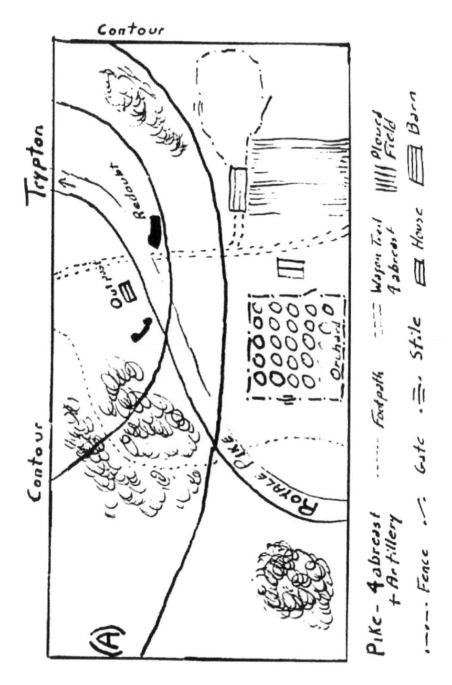

It is also permissible for the defender to enter the field with only a portion of his forces committed, the balance held in reserve and due to enter at a given point on a given turn. Again, this should be clearly indicated. It is suggested that sealed envelopes marked with the appropriate move number be used.

In 'timing', a battle against a day's march, assume two table moves equal one hour's march.

If Largemouthana wins the battle, the city is his.

So long as hostilities between Tryptagolia and Largemouthana continue, any country desiring to attack either would be limited to attacking one colony or city in one game month.

Forces in Battle

Except for captured artillery, the rules should never permit a force larger than a Division by a quarter nor less than three quarters of a Division be used in battles. A victorious Division should have the half Division 'bonus' added to its survivors immediately following the battle, thus if it is attacked by another of the enemy's Divisions it will not be forced to withdraw from the field unless the additional does not bring its total men to at least three quarters of a Division, hardly likely since battles leaving less than a quarter Division to the victor would be a battle of mutual annihilation with no winner!

In battles for cities, the onus is on the Attackers. So long as the Defenders prevent the Attackers passing their position with at least a quarter of a Division the Attackers have not won the battle!

Map Movement

A record of daily movement outside one's homeland or colony should be kept and reported to the umpire on a regular basis. These reports should account for Attack Divisions, Fleets and the shifting of captured artillery.

Roads speed movement of troops. A rule-of-thumb is offered:

Troops march 20 miles per day on roads, 10 miles off.

Ships sail 50 miles per day.

Detached Cavalry and Light Infantry units march 30 miles per day on roads, 15 miles off.

Detached messenger Brigs sail 75 miles per day.

Couriers ride 50 miles per day on roads, 30 miles off.

Matters pertaining to ships operating on rivers or lakes may be decided when a game is organised. Generally ships might be allowed to sail to the second contour of the Schmerd River in Tryptagolia and through Lake Bile. A constant river sailing distance of 20 miles daily is recommended.

It is realised that this is insufficient information to begin an 'international' game immediately. This section is designed as a guide to those interested.

Photo 21: Austrian Line Cuirassiers charging Polish Lancers of French Imperial Guard

Points Value Games

A study of the major battles in the Napoleonic wars shows the fallacy of 'total annihilation' wargames. Even after Waterloo, Napoleon had enough survivors to field a formidable army had *Le Tondu* not lost the backing of the French populace. Of course, Ney's 'We have no army' speech before the Chamber of Peers on June 2 didn't help much!

But my point is this: wargames of total annihilation are unrealistic and seldom a measure of the skill of either player. Merely to place troops on the table and butt into each other until one survives requires no skill or imagination - true, the more skilful player will usually win, but this is still no test.

A scoring system based on combat units, position on the field, supply, etc., should be established and maintained. Using the lowest common denominator, let us assume one has the 20 man company as the basic unit: let one line company represent 20 points; a line grenadier company represent 30 points, and a guard company, 40 points. A horse gun could then represent 10 points; a 6-pounder, 30 points, and a howitzer, 50 points.

Supply factors would enter in. Assuming a game move to represent one hour's actual time, the forces would have to be fed every sixth move and would be permitted to miss one meal; a second meal or supply unit missed would force surrender due to the lack of supplies. Each supply wagon would be capable of carrying certain amount of supplies, both food and ammunition. Each unit would have to be within a certain distance of a supply dump or wagon in order to receive supplies.

Strategic points would have varying values, both in supply and control points. An important intersection might carry 100 control and 50 supply points while a village held 100 supply and 50 control points. Once levelled by artillery fire, the village would lose all control value and its supplies would be assumed destroyed unless removed by wagons.

Using a scoring basis of some sort, games could be set for a maximum amount of playing time or a maximum number of moves, at the end of the allotted time, the 'score' could then be counted and the winner declared on the basis of total points. Prisoners then take on new importance as points added to the captor's total score.

This facet of the game bears individual development. It would be easy, but quite presumptuous, for me to draw up an arbitrary table.

Wargaming is a test of skill. Here again, the importance of making decisions in a limited amount of time becomes apparent. If one is playing a game scheduled for six hours, one wants to get in as many moves as possible in order to gain control of as much territory or 'points value' as possible.

Photo 22: Prussian Landwehr surprising Austrian Artillery

Photo 23: French Grenadiers a Cheval attacking Prussian Line at Enfilade

Addendum: Model General's Club Matrix Systems

Melee Deployment Matrix (MDM) (Adopted 10 July 1963)

By Gerard De Gre, Secretary-General MGC

1.   The Melee Department Matrix (MDM) is used to determine combat effects of troops in melee on the basis of combat decisions simultaneously made by both commanders.

2.   MDM is employed only after opposing units have been moved into contact and represents a <u>theoretical</u> local tactical deployment of the units engaged, so it is not necessary to actually redeploy the model units in melee combat.

3.   <u>EQUIPMENT</u> <u>REQUIRED</u>: Each commander requires a set of six Melee Deployment Indicators (MDI). The simplest method is to make two sets of index cards, each set typed or lettered as follows: FLANKING; SQUARE; LINE; PINCER; or WITHDRAWAL. A very satisfactory set of MDI can be made by using wooden Anagram[7] letter blocks making two sets, each consisting of: F, S, C, L, P, or W.

4.   <u>PROCEDURE</u>: Melee having been joined, each commander selects a MDI placing the indicator face-down before him. Both then turn the MDI up for the particular melee being adjudicated. Results are then assessed. This procedure is repeated for each melee.

5.   The Melee Deployment Matrix operates on the assumption that certain tactical deployments are always superior to certain others. In general, with the exception of the WITHDRAWAL option, each Deployment is superior to two others and inferior to two others:

FLANKING is superior to SQUARE and to LINE

SQUARE is superior to COLUMN and to PINCER

COLUMN is superior to FLNKING and to PINCER

LINE is superior to SQUARE and to COLUMN

PINCER is superior to LINE and to FLANKING

WITHDRAWAL is successful when opponent chooses SQUARE or LINE; it fails when

Opponent chooses FLANKING or PINCER; it succeeds when opponent chooses COLUMN,

---

[7] Or Scrabble letter tiles

But COLUMN pursues for a new melee deployment. Withdrawal deployments, when successful, are one infantry move to the rear, optional facing

6. Definition of the various tactical deployments:

SQUARE (SQ) symbolises either a defence in square or a phalanx assault, and is the best response to an anticipated Pincer envelopment or Column assault.

COLUMN (CO) represents a rapid oblique movement in Column which hits the weak pivoting point of a Flanking or Pincer movement.

PINCER (P) is an enveloping pincer movement which traps either a Line or a Flanking deployment in enfilade.

FLANKING (F) indicates a flanking movement which hits either a Square or a Line formation on its flank.

LINE (LI) presents the widest front to its opponents, bringing the full effect of its weapons to bear on a Column or Square.

WITHDRAWAL (W) represents the attempt to extricate units in melee by falling back in an orderly manner to the rear. It is successful when the opponent has deployed himself into Line or Square, but is always cut off by Flanking and Pincer movements.

7. The Matrix Table in Adjudication of Melee Combat:

a) Force in Superior Deployment destroys one per each combat unit superior in NUMBERS, and therefore one unit for every two units in Superior Deployment (one-half loss forces retreat of one unit)

1. Force remaining with lower number of units retreats remaining units two moves towards the rear, and faces towards the rear.

2. If number of units remaining are equal, then units in inferior DEPLOYMENT retreat two moves towards the rear, and face in that direction. Retreated units may be wheeled, but not moved on the following moving turn.

b) When Deployments are the same (e.g. Line versus Line), the force with the smaller NUMBER of combat units loses all units, and the larger force loses an equal number LESS one for each combat unit superior in numbers.

1. If the number of units is the same, then the force enjoying superior PROTECTION wins the melee, opponent losing all units, and the winner loses one less per protection factor.

2. If the number of units and protection are equal, then the heavier force (e.g. that with more cavalry or elite units) wins the melee,

destroying all of its opponent's units, the heavier force losing one unit less.

3. If the number of units is the same, and neither is superior in protection or type of units, then the melee continues into the following turn, all units continue to be engaged, and new supporting units and artillery fire may be committed, and each may select new simultaneous deployments.

ARTILLERY FIRE MATRIX

(Adopted October 5th 1963)

1. The Artillery Fire Matrix (AFM) is used to determine artillery hits by the designation of zones of fire within target squares. It is employed normally on battlefields which have been divided into squares.

2. Following the move of attacking units, both the attacker and the defender designate artillery target squares, placing shell fire markers therein.

3. Each square is divided theoretically into four zones for the purpose of adjudication of effect of fire:

A: CENTRE FRONT
B: RIGHT FLANK
C: REAR
D: LEFT FLANK

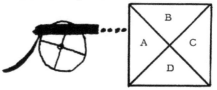

4. For each round of fire, the Gun Captain selects by written concealed orders* a zone of fire within the target SQUARE. He may fire several batteries into the same zone in order to increase his effect; or he may cover more than one zone in order to increase his probabilities of hitting the targets, by bringing several batteries to bear on different zones of the same square.

5. The commander of the troops being fired upon simultaneously issues written concealed orders* for the location of his forces in a specific zone in the target square: ALL OF HIS UNITS must be ordered into the same ZONE.

6. When both are ready, the previously designated target zones are compared with the theoretical zone location ordered by the commander of the troops being fired upon. A HIT IS REGISTERED IF THE ZONE OF FIRE CORRESPONDS TO THE ZONE OF LOCATION OF TARGET UNITS. It is not necessary to move the units into the actual zone designated, it is assumed that they have been ordered into that section of the target square. Normally, one round destroys one unit in the target zone; one half effect versus protected targets except at half-range.

7. A dice roll may be used to determine effect on MIXED targets:

2-3 Hit on Infantry or lowest value unit in zone

    4 Hit on Lt. Infantry, Elite Guard Infantry or above
    5 Hit on Cavalry, Elite Light Infantry or above
    6 Hit on Elite Guards, Cavalry, Wagon and Crew or above
    1 Hit on artillery unit and crew, or any other unit of personnel or material; an incendiary hit on buildings, woods, bridges, forts, etc.

Note: The dice roll is used only against mixed targets or to determine possible incendiary effect. When firing at a square containing only one troop type (e.g. Infantry only), then no dice roll is needed.

*Anagram letters A, B, C or D can be used here with good effect.

Play in good health and companionship!

John Candler